loss of soul:
burnout

To Frankie

kelly walker

Kelly Walker

KW Publications©

Canadian Cataloguing in Publication Data

Walker, Kelly, 1941-
Loss of soul : burnout

Includes bibliographical references and index.

ISBN 0-9680315-0-1

1. Burn out (Psychology). I. Title.

BF481.W35 1995	155.9'042	C95-920890-9

Published in Canada by KW Publication
715-80 Front Street East
Toronto, Ontario Canada
M5E 1T4

Printed by the Aylmer Express Limited, Aylmer Ontario, Canada

Cover & Design: Tony Sorbera

Photo: V.Tony Hauser

To Ray Harsant
for
his encouragement
his wisdom
his friendship

My song is love unknown,
My Saviour's love to me,
Love to the loveless shown,
That they might lovely be.
O who am I,
That for my sake
My Lord should take
Frail flesh and die?

John N. Ireland, 1925

Loss of Soul:*burnout*

Contents

Loss of Soul:*burnout*

Preface

For most of my life I have lived with a very large script that read: YOU CANNOT... This included writing books!!! I began writing this book with great reluctance. It was born out of requests from many people to make my reflections available to them in print. I am very grateful to them for the final push. I was always afraid that someone would ridicule what I had to say if it were in print. To speak it was one thing. To write it down was another. I cannot skip town after this one!

I have written this book for you. I have written it for the kind of people who can't be bothered with footnotes or complicated notions. I have written it for those who often find themselves living at the edge of the precipice and don't really want to jump. I have written it for those who yearn for wholeness, for those who still have a faint memory of what it was to be happy.

This book has been designed for you to *live with*. Please abuse its pages with a pencil. There are large margins at the sides for your reflections. There are a few blank pages here and there for you to scribble or draw or reflect on - or just to look at!

This is not a scientific work. I have purposely not given footnotes and page references. I have included in the bibliography the books on the subject of burnout that I like best. Many other authors have done the research. I have attempted to synthesize and harmonize a number of disciplines with my own thoughts to create this work.

Most books on burnout have very little to do with spirituality. I believe that the *real* issue is there. We are a generation that has too readily sold our souls to the company store. We need to recover them.

The process of recovery is long and hard. Reading this book will not do it for you. Reading all the books I suggest will not do it. But if you decide to get on a path and stick to it, you will change. I suggest you do this work with another person or with a few others.

This earth needs us to recover our health in order for the planet to survive. *Environmental* clean-up will only be valid if our *personal, human* clean-up is happening at the same time. I hope this book will contribute to that programme a bit.

I have written this book with references to Hebrew and Christian mythology. I have not done this to convert anybody. These stories come out of my own Christian faith which gives passion to my dreams and which undergirds all of my life. I believe that the creation story of Israel and the desert episodes of Jesus of Nazareth are universal enough to be of benefit to anyone. I know, as well, that the other world religions capture the same energy in their stories. I have chosen the ones I know well as they give deep meaning to what goes on in burnout or any depression.

I believe that the West's present socio-economic world view is destructive. It promises freedom. It delivers slavery. In order to survive as humans, we must create a new world order.

Each nation has value. We must learn to respect our own national gifts and use them to contribute to the common good. For us all to become alike is foolish.

I am a Canadian. I am not an American. The struggle of the people of Canada with our varied cultures is an icon for the world at this time. My country could be saved by the First Nations' soul recovery. My country could be saved by our people learning both French and English. We can choose to listen and to speak to each other or to live back to back in denial.

I am a male. I cannot bear sexism.

I have tried to avoid writing his/her because I find it distracting. If you need to replace a his with a her in your reading, do so. I find it confusing to just scramble them. I've generally opted for the male form.

Please enjoy this journey of discovery with me. I hope you will understand why I believe that burnout is about *loss of soul* and that recovery is fundamentally about *soul recovery*. I also hope that these pages help you find the courage and the energy you need to grow to be an exciting human being. This is the dream of this earth - to produce creatures of delight and dignity.

To continue reading these pages is dangerous. You might spark a human revolution.

Scribble, day dream, wonder, paint, sing, dance and welcome in the new day that we all dream about.

Toronto, October 7, 1995

Loss of Soul:*burnout*

Introduction

Going Down The Road

It had been one of those seasons that required "heroics" just to make it through. At least they were heroics in my mind. I was 40. I had been a Dominican Friar for 20 years. I had been ordained to the priesthood on August 10, 1968, (six years after entering), and the next day put on a life script that would prepare me for the morning of September 26, 1981. I was driving up the Don Valley Parkway in Toronto at 06:30. I had been preaching to some nuns in Peterborough (1 1/2 hours northeast). During the time with the nuns, I decided that I HAD TO attend to the wedding of my favourite kid in the parish. Thus, I had to travel to Burlington (2 1/2 hours west) to do the rehearsal on Thursday evening, return to the nuns for 08:00 Friday morning, leave Friday night to do the wedding in Burlington on Saturday morning, attend the reception and leave for Peterborough on Sunday morning to preach to the nuns at 08:00. Got the picture? That was the script I had accepted for my salvation in August 1968. "Be there for anyone whenever they want you and forget about yourself."

The tears were so copious at 06:30 as I was driving north on the Don Valley Parkway, that I had to pull over to the shoulder of the road. I screamed out as I slammed on the brakes, "I CAN'T STAND ALL THIS ADULATION WITH NO INTIMACY!" I continued to cry.

1

My life flashed before my eyes like the action cards that I flipped as a boy in order to see a scene. The major image that hit me was one of *giving without end*. That's the way it appeared to me. Generosity without boundaries. It was only after many years of intense therapy that I was able to realize that it really was *self-centredness without end*. But it bore the noble armour of charity. I was misguided, trapped and alone.

During the few minutes that ensued before I re-mounted my sturdy Ford and continued north, I proclaimed out of the blue, "YOU HAVE LEFT!" Never before had I entertained the thought of leaving my beloved Dominicans with any seriousness. Surely, I had thought of having my own place, my own money, an intimate relationship, children. But never had the thought taken a true shape in my mind. I thought I was happy. I had been elected Prior three times. My life was gracious, generous and loving. The community was sane and prospering. The Order was open, compassionate and relevant. Where was this coming from? Where could it lead? But somehow, in those few brief moments, I knew that I had left the Order and my life as I had known it.

A few years later I was re-reading my favourite book by Sheldon Kopp called <u>IF YOU MEET THE BUDDHA ON THE ROAD, KILL HIM</u>. On the introductory page I found that I had written this:

> kelly walker
> 1977
> phase II.

Not Fr. Kelly Walker O.P. but kelly walker.

I BEGAN LEAVING IN 1977!!! The four years were years for the passage from "KNOWLEDGE TO ACKNOWLEDGE". It took time for my "eco-system" to *get it!*

I continued to cry as I went along the highway to the monastery of nuns. But I got there. I preached at 08:00 as I was supposed to.

The days that followed were eventful. Angels appeared from all corners to be with me. Terry Collins, Bishop Doyle, Albert Leering, Ron and Anika Pileski, Bill Lambie, Hildegard Schmidt-Malo, Kevin Flynn, Georges Perreault, Jean-Marc Gay, Peter and Pat Robinson,

George Kern, Paul Franceschini and Deirdre Plomer. They held me, embraced my story, cried with me and asked me the right questions. I quickly began to process the crisis and decided with the shared wisdom that little by little I should move out on my own.

During the months that preceeded this banner day, I was noticeably absent from the life of the community. I was late for appointments. I double and triple booked. I was breathless, out of control, suicidal. I was dangerous on the highway. I sometimes lived events but forgot that I had been there. I forgot information. Ideas slipped in and out of my mind. I had been vomiting, crying, having diarrhea, aching, suffering from blurred vision, slurring speech and experiencing shortness of breath.

People noticed. Some even courageously spoke to me. The Dominican brothers and sisters gave me silent messages but our deep respect for each member's honour, dignity and freedom kept them from trying to interfere with me.

I had begun to ask myself what I could possibly do. Would I sweep this event under the rug and get on with it? That was certainly the script that I had lived. No. I knew that I would re-live the event at 50 if I did so. Could I move out? I had never lived on my own, so that was a threat. Should I see a therapist? But I was one! Could I disappoint everybody and become Kelly again? Had I ever really been Kelly? Who was he?

The doctors strongly suggested that I cancel everything. For a month? No. For good! But I was booked for three years!!! I began to phone and write to cancel my life. I thought it would have been the end of my life. Now I know that had I not cancelled my work assignments, I would have cancelled out my life.

I did move out. I went to Stratford, Ontario and lived above the Old Prune Restaurant. I thought the name was appropriate. I had my own little apartment for the first time. I painted, wallpapered, found furniture, moved my piano in and cried my way into a new life. I lost weight. I lived in fear and deepest guilt and tried desperately to imagine a life. I lived on the little stipend that the Order was able to give me. I went to psycho-therapy with Hildegard Schmidt-Malo and shiatsu with Junzo Kokubo and Helen Taylor weekly in Toronto and tried to recover my body and my soul. I began the Nicholas Technique exercise programme with Ellen Field Balkan in order to help me breathe and stretch. My designer friend, Sybil Casey took me shopping in Yorkville to buy new snazzy clothes. I bought pots and pans at any store I could. I bought sheets that matched and a duvet and a bed. I started to get an idea about what an adult male life outside a total institution could look like. I began to feel "ordinary". I had always worn a "uniform" of some kind. Now I had no uniform, no title, no family and no money. I also had no work - a reality that had given me my most significant identity - and in the same vein, nobody to need me. This was withdrawal. Who would I be?

I have strong memories of tears. Tears of guilt. Tears of terror. Tears of loneliness. I had never slept alone in a place before. As soon as the lights would go out I would start to hyperventilate. I couldn't even sleep. I was frantic in my solitude. I HAD NO IDENTITY. I had never really owned anything and felt guilty about everything I purchased and afraid of the judgement that others would put on my little possessions.

In the springtime I moved back to Toronto. I felt that the Church would not want me there as I was an embarrassment to them, but at the same time I had to be where I knew people. I found a wonderful new place to live above the Gage mansion in Wychwood Park. Nancy Forrest helped me create "my home" with colour and good design. I settled into a life of "people without end" who came to see who I was becoming. I felt as though a life was forming. There was, however, to be no work for some time.

Mary O'Hara, the premier Irish singer and harpist had heard me sing in Halifax a year prior to my breakdown and had heard on the grapevine that I had left the monastery. One evening in July, Mary called and invited me to be her accompanist and to sing with her in a concert at the Royal Ontario Museum Concert Hall. Hope! This was followed by more work with Mary throughout Canada.

That same summer, I got a job playing piano at La Castille's "Bull and Bush" cocktail lounge in Mississauga. I learned everything George Gershwin and Cole Porter ever wrote in order to make it in the entertainment industry. Life was beginning to happen for me. Mary Baier and Joan Donovan, my Dominican sisters were able to lend me money and I purchased a Schimmel grand piano from Hans Mueller. Life began to take shape for me.

Life at the bar was uncomfortable. Visits from old parishioners, fellow theologues, strangers and new friends changed a bar into Kelly's living room. The press caught on. There were articles about the transition. Everybody knew. The phantom of the bishops weighed heavily on my heart. The guilt increased as the new identity struggled for its own breath. But somehow it worked. With the love and support of Ron and Donna Richardson and my god-daughter Jennifer, I began to create a family of my own. Kelly the entertainer emerged. Kelly the friend. Kelly the poet and troubadour. It was working.

The *process of transition* is the most difficult. Change is not so hard. But that sacred in-between time is frightening. I knew I needed a fallow time. I knew that plunging into something could ruin the whole picture. But someone who had become a "human *doing*" was having a mighty hard time just "*being*". The monastic experience did not prepare one for the perilous journey that the end of the 20th century would propose as normal. Stability is not the norm in the latter half of the 20th century. Flexibility and creativity is. That was new.

Work with Mary O'Hara continued. TV in England with Mary and Liona Boyd. My own concerts booked through my faithful and fine manager Chris O'Toole. And the albums - thanks to Paul Zaza and Bill King and Dominic Morrissey. I was beginning to have my own face.

But the burnout was still lingering in my soul. I was lonely, afraid and without a land of my own. I still felt like a foreigner, a betrayer sought after by the kings.

I was considered an "invalid Christian witness" by the reigning bishop at the time and was dis-allowed from having anything to do with Catholic school teachers - a grace-filled task that had been my bread and butter. The current papal legislation made it impossible to have any Catholic post. So, I had to play at the bar just to pay the rent. A local bishop demeaned my new life and referred to me in public and professional settings as "that piano player". That was hard as I felt so confused about my breakdown. I also felt unwelcome in the Catholic parish and so began to seek God in the communities of the Anglican Church.

It was there that I met my wife to be. The need for legitimacy, for honour, for security and acceptance pushed me in the direction of marriage. And such a gracious and loving woman made the journey possible. She saved me. I accepted. I shouldn't have. My journey was not yet completed. The marriage lasted for seven years until my search for soul pushed me out of it.

Mid-life is a time for new awakenings. Crisis. Yes. Awakening to the TRUTH often causes us to abandon hitherto valid life scripts in honour of new truth. What a pity that this often causes deep wounds in those around us. Perhaps that is why we ought to go to the desert for a period of time. Alone.

It is out of this journey in search of soul that these pages follow. I have listened to my own journey and as a counsellor, therapist and priest, I have listened to thousands on *their* journey. The journey itself is worth it. The pain is part of the adventure. The way is perilous and long. But freedom and peace is the reward.

> Nel mezzo del cammin di nostra vita
> mi ritrovai per una selva oscura
> che la diritta via era smarrita…
>
> In the middle of life's journey
> I found myself in a dark forest
> the way ahead obscured.
>
> Dante

Loss of Soul:*burnout*

Chapter One

Loss Of Soul

I seem to be floating above my body, watching myself work and look after the whole world. This can't be real. I slip back and forth constantly.
Adult child of an Alzheimer patient

Sometimes I feel as though I am little by little disappearing. The phones keep ringing. The requests for help keep coming in. I feel as though I am not here. I get scared that I'll screw up.
Social Worker

I've been living through a period where I have not been able to distinguish dream from reality. I fear that I am going crazy, although I seem to be able to get to and from work.
Minister

Sometimes I feel as though I'm on a train. I don't know where it's going and I don't have the energy to get off.
Professor

Loss of Soul: *burnout*

I feel like I've been turned into a liquid from a solid. Everyone has had a turn sucking me up into a syringe and I'm trapped inside the barrel. My potency has weakened and I'm leaking out the needle, absorbed into nowhere.
Nurse

I felt as though my self was sucking my self into myself. I was disappearing!
Kelly Walker

My soul began to push my whole eco-system into spasm.
Kelly Walker

What good does it do you to gain the whole world and lose your soul?
Jesus of Nazareth

Soul

Soul is the energy that surrounds and undergirds all reality. It is the breath that breathes us into being and at the same time sustains our existence. It is invisible yet takes the shape of everything that comes into this terrestrial sphere. It is that melody that gives unity to everything that is and was and will be. It is deepest mystery - as a string linking all the pearls into one strand. It is at one and the same time the dancer and the dance, the singer and the song, the painter and the painting. It is beyond all definition and yet is open to description without limit. We are both given it and are it. We give birth to it in others and assure its radiance in the universe by our being, our doing and our having. Soul is a moment of the eternity and being of the Creator. It is the very breath of God. No one has it completely, yet each being is completely one with the Creator.

Our existence is defined by soul. Our individuality is due to it. But also our communality is from it. It is about the shape our energy defines or confines itself in at each phase of our existence. It is how we incarnate in each moment, how we manifest, how we extend in time and space. It has no limitations and can go backward and forward, up and down, in and out and beyond. It is about eternity and the now.

Geist, nephesh, anima, psyche, prana are all words that have been used to describe what we mean when we say SOUL. From the dawning of time to the New Age, people have used some word to describe that which is at the core of our being, that which animates us, which gives us meaning, which links us to all that is. Words, symbols and stories have been sought to explicate that which is entirely mysterious to us. (See Phil Cousineau Ed., SOUL, An Archeology). Our word *soul* has its roots in the Old English *sawol* and the Icelandic *sala*.

Disappearing

Jesus' words about soul loss have sparked a great deal of reflection over the past 2000 years. Most often they were interpreted within the context of material wealth as a detriment to soul growth. I am not at all convinced that he was pushing poverty. I believe his words about soul loss were about giving yourself over to some reality and allowing that reality to take over your life, to become bigger than yourself to the point that it consumes your total energy. *You* begin to fade as *it* overwhelms *you*.

This concept has had greater and greater meaning for me as a result of my last twelve years in private practice working with people who visited me to deal with *burnout*. So many spoke about "disappearing". I can clearly remember driving in the car as a young Dominican and experiencing that I was *somewhere else* and *outside my body*. I had invested my total being in work, caring, worrying, organizing and governing. There was *no more me*. I had no intimacy with myself! I had begun to disappear from my self.

Initially stories about disappearing seemed delusional. I had melted this *disappearing* into the barrel of burnout symptoms and continued treating their behaviour as a reality that simply needed some deep modification. But as these stories began to come up again and again in sessions, I began to take them more seriously. It struck me: THESE PEOPLE ARE TALKING ABOUT DISAPPEARING! They are feeling that they are NOT HERE. I knew that I had experienced that feeling but had not been able to articulate it until sometime after my 1981 breakdown. My clients gave me the vocabulary (how often this is the case) to help me describe what I could only later speak about as "soul loss".

In the years prior to Thomas Moore's CARE FOR THE SOUL, I would have hesitated writing or speaking about the concept of "soul". I am convinced now that the term has validity for our discussion once it has been cleansed of the moralistic overtones that so many of us were raised with.

Disappearing Is Burnout Is Soul Loss

Soul loss is the true expression for what happens when the *whole eco-system* is depleted. It is soul loss that happens when the good, generous and often very successful women and men (in most aspects of their life) begin to *fall apart* from the INSIDE OUT. Generally it is the outer shell that is the last to break down. The inner breakdown has been going on for some time before it appears.

I felt compelled to write about burnout in these terms rather than in a "fix-it" fashion because I simply do not believe that the condition can be cured by time -, food -, systems - or relationship - *management*. The issue is far more serious and can only be resolved through deep soul (or spiritual) recovery. Anything else is fluff. (See Carol Fassel, WORKING OURSELVES TO DEATH).

Breath

Breath is the fundamental animating principle in all living creatures. Without it we perish. The Ancients speak of soul in terms of breath using such words a pneuma, ruah, spiritus. It was the power which came from somewhere else and which was expelled at death. "He breathed his last breath" is an expression we employ to talk about death. Breath-less is a word which comes from the mouth of people who have given themselves away. They speak of being "out of breath". In their frenzy they are both physically and spiritually trying to embrace the world. Good intentions. Bad methodology.

To be healthy and effective we must have good breathing. Every athlete knows that a first principle of success is good breath-monitoring. Every singer or actor knows it. Every acting manual has many chapters on breathing techniques. When it was still playing on Broadway, the cast of A CHORUS LINE would spend an hour before every performance doing NICHOLAS TECHNIQUE breathing and stretching exercises and then went on stage with the energy that true living requires.

We notice that when a person is in a state of depression, his breathing is shallow. This condition can be changed by the introduction of either internal or external stimuli which will engage the spirit. (See Alexander Louwen, DEPRESSION AND THE BODY). Low-grade depression is accompanied by very shallow breathing. The depression can be broken by vigorous breathing.

Jim was a man in his early 40's. He was the personnel director of a very large company which had downsizing as a major 90's event. Jim was to "man" the process. He was the son of a very zealous but never too successful salesman. His father had died of a heart attack at mid-life and had left Jim with a life-script that proclaimed that he too would never quite "make it". All the same, he was to work hard, be faithful and retire with a pension. That was the main goal that had been passed on. Jim did work hard, had integrity and creativity, was faithful to a very dysfunctional company. At the same time he lived with an almost certain sense that he would never be able to retire from the company. He lived with a triple script.

(i) Someone would shoot him at work since he was the "main executioner".

(ii) He would arrive at work to be told by another manager that his job was finished.

(iii) He would go to work and have a heart attack and die - like his dad.

This over-hanging shadow was like a weight on his chest. He could not get his breath. Often he hyperventilated. He often arrived for his session late, out of breath and with skin that matched his grey flannel suit. When confronted with the pain of letting people go, he would again go into a breathless state and nearly faint. He also felt that he was "withering away". He suffered weight loss, diarrhea, and hyperventilation. No wonder he worried about having a heart attack and dying like his dad!

Henry was a designer. Successful. Handsome. Gregarious. He had more clients than he knew what to do with. He was defined by the number of clients he had. He began in his early 50's to "unglue". Hence his need for some therapy. He had tried all the management courses, played at golf religiously, joined the squash club, and kept abreast with his various clubs. In his car he had a phone, a computer and a fax. Never once in the year that we worked together was he on time. He called me every time to say that he was going to be late. Several times he called in the last half hour to say that he "would be there". That he had to pay and that he had 10 minutes for a session did not seem to bother him. He always arrived PANTING. On several occasions I asked him bluntly, "Do you want to die?" He replied, "No!" and we continued.

He had also created an office that was breathless. Every member of the staff assured the emperor that he did have clothes on and every member served him well as a co-dependent. When I asked him to consider not taking on new clients he assured me that HE could stop but that his team might have difficulty. They all had the disease. He needed to change before they could get their breath again.

In the end he decided he didn't have time for the sessions and off he went on the perilous path that has led so many of our generation to an early grave.

These men spoke to me at length of losing their souls. They had the things that they wanted but they no longer were able to grasp themselves. THEY COULD NOT CATCH THEIR BREATH AND WERE BEGINNING TO DISAPPEAR!

Identity

Soul is also that life-principle that makes me to be me and not another. A person with a grounded "self", an animated "child", is one who is able to delight in his own being and is not defined mainly in relation to another. Indeed, every human has definition in-relationship-to the world as well as to other humans. But the principal source of a person's being is the "soul" from which activity emanates.

When one becomes defined by "doing" rather than by "being", trouble occurs. It is so common in our civilization to define self by occupation, role, status or material possessions. These, of course, define us as servants to a system which "needs" us to lose self in its favour. Oddly enough, this happens as much in the world of healing, religion and the arts as in the more obvious jobs that support capitalism. It is not hard to lose one's soul in the pseudo-identity of "giving" without boundaries that public ministry brings with it.

Creativity

The aspects of soul that speak of creativity, imagination and spirit are those realities that make us very attractive to others. They are the major reasons one of us is chosen for a task over and above others. These are essentially "human" characteristics.

Human beings have the innate ability to 'go beyond', to stretch - seeking new terrain, dreaming, intuiting. We are able to do the un-imaginable. What was a spark in the imagination a generation ago is household for us now. It is energy emanating from the soul that allows us to communicate globally, instantly. It is SIMPLY human. To fly to the moon is only phase one of a much more elaborate dream of humankind. Just watch STAR TRECK! The next generations will look back on our fantasies and blush at their primitiveness.

We are "stardust", "golden", Woodstock proclaimed. But for our survival we have to "get ourselves back to the garden". Creativity gone amuck, creativity pushed beyond its own limits somehow makes us disappear. We DO have limits, despite the Anthony Robbin's hype. We do happen to be human and not full of boundless energy (another "soul" word). We still need rest and food and time for self in order to be able to do the boundless creative stuff that we are made of/for.

Humour

The Latin word "humor" means liquid, water. It is another aspect of soul, specific (we think) to HUMAN (from HUMUS). JOY, LAUGHTER, SMILE. These are realities that we live/die for. Our stories, our songs, our temples are about this. The Inuit word for making love is the same as "to giggle", "to make laughter". In fact, as a little boy, I was taught to call my penis my "little giggle". Was that female humour, or was there a connection within the psyche of the English language?

One of our biggest industries in the 20th century world is that of entertainment. Its deepest dream is to bring us INTO the reality of the most humorous, the most human of the experiences. Three dimensions are not even enough. We want to "get inside" the very realities that inform us. We do not just want to experience humour and the human story. WE HAVE AN ENORMOUS THIRST IN OUR GENERATION TO BE IT!!! Thus the great lust for drug in any form, whether it be heroin or "endorphin release" in any way we can get it. As we approach the 21st century, to be a spectator is not sufficient. WE WANT TO BE IT! NOW! Virtual reality; virtually, but not quite!

It is clear that as the human is consumed with hunger for unbounded work, care and giving, he begins to lose his humour. Sadness takes over. Cynicism and jaded humour expose a lost soul. Often humour is present but in very sick forms. Those forms of humour have become almost "normative" in an addictive society. Our sitcoms and comedians are a witness to this. Humourless, frozen religion, business practice and "law"(rather than "peace") enforcement manifests this, too. Hyper-serious rather than mystical therapy reigns as well. The *crazy* has no role in this society for manifesting the inner truth of reality. Serious humanity fails to see the numinous, the dream, the totally-other as having any bearing on reality. As a human can lose soul, so can businesses, churches and the entertainment-machine. Sad.

Communion

The mystery of communion is also an aspect of soul. We are part of a universal being. We are never defined ALONE. Human is inter-connected with everything that is and was and will be. The global village that we live in is only part of its total reality. We are as much part of our elders as we are of our children. The deep work done in this generation on addiction and dysfunctional families has only touched the tip of the iceberg. (See Alice Miller, FOR YOUR OWN GOOD). We are intimately related not only to humans but to all aspects of life on the planet and beyond.

One mystical moment in my life happened when I was at Kai Luum in the Yucatan Peninsula in Mexico in 1983. I had been drinking "café Toronto" with some Canadian friends (it had coffee in it, too). I happened to trip (or at least stumble) on my way back to my tent one evening. There were myriads of stars above me in the endless black of the sky. They were inches above my mind. I cried out the mystical expression, "I AM PART OF THEM!!!" I cried at the truth of the proclamation. In a sick mode I would have proclaimed that they were PART OF ME.

With loss of soul, little by little the human isolates himself from the garden and then from the food and then from the people as the addiction to "doing" takes over. All inter-connectedness goes and the inflated ego floats off into nothingness. We disappear!

Loss of Soul:*burnout*

Chapter Two

Tardemah

Hebrew literature is full of myths that come out of the experiences of this ancient people. The "first story" in Genesis 2, speaks of human made of humus (ha'adam from ha'adamah). This is a primary characteristic of this new being that begins life as a non-sexually defined being created by YAHWEH. Creator takes ha'adamah and breathes the "breath of life" into this creature and gives IT a living soul (nephesh). This creature, the myth states, is the very IKON of the Creator. But there was something lacking in this being. No hitherto created reality could assuage the thirst of ha'adam for communion. So Creator puts ha'adam into a TARDEMAH (a deep, dark slumber/time within which transformation takes place) and out of that time/space emerged a new creature. From that point the myth speaks of Adam and Eve (ish and ishah).

What we can learn from this part of the myth (the Hebrew FIRST STORY) is that without tardemah there can be no new life.

Mark was sent to me because his mother was at her wits end to try to help her son out of a deep and recurring depression. He had been to his family doctor who prescribed some drugs as a possible way of dealing with the inner confusion and sadness of this 28 year old man.

Mark went home and tried the drug. He felt uncomfortable with this substance and threw it down the toilet. He then went to a local psychiatric institution and was asked by the psychiatrist in charge if he'd mind being "watched" by a few other doctors. He freaked out and ran out the door.

"What are *you* going to do?" he politely asked me."Nothing!" I replied; "*you* are." I asked him to remain in the depression. I wanted him to "go down there" and get words, images, icons, smells and inklings of what went on there. I also told him that as his elder I would go down with him and help him "get it". I told him two stories: the first about the creation in Genesis 2 and the second about Jesus of Nazareth in the desert. He listened. He smiled and with a smirk on his face said,"That is the craziest thing I've ever heard." "Maybe" was my reply. "Try it?" "OK, I guess!"

He did. He did hear voices, sounds, images and little by little with my help emerged from the darkness.

The story of Jesus is the same one as the TARDEMAH story and Mark's story. His baptism in the Jordan by his religious-reformer cousin John must have been pivotal for a middle-aged man from an orthodox religious family. By this gesture he decided to publicly renounce the "temple" and all that it stood for in terms of religious addiction and focus. He embraced a form of religion that reflected the prophetic reform of the prophets away from "forms" and "law" and towards the "inner" recovery of soul and integration with the world.

After his baptism he is lead "by the Spirit" into the desert where he spends 40 days and 40 nights being tempted by the Devil to put on the "pseudo self" of power, ownership and magic. He rejects it. But not without horrendous struggle. Nikos Kazantzakis' description of Jesus in THE LAST TEMPTATION OF CHRIST makes it fairly clear that he "goes crazy" during this episode of mid-life. Who wouldn't? Is it not NORMAL to do this at this age?

This is another *model* for us of what goes on in major growth. TARDEMAH is normal. We go into the dark times. Rollo May says that *daemon* is any power that becomes 'as another person' within us.

We know them. They are our compulsions, our addictions, our pseudo selves that falsely define us at various times of our life. They deaden our souls and create superficial joy in us, superficial power and authority. But we NEED these compulsive behaviours to ease the pain that dwells within our sad souls. Yet, if we begin to BECOME them, we begin to disappear.

In this desert-time of struggle and decision, Jesus was sent angels by the Creator, for consolation and support - "lest he dash his foot against a stone".

So trust. You too will be given angels. It is part of the creation.

Many of us come out of a generation that had little place for "breakdown". The response to breakdown most often was "pull up your socks and get on with it"; "smile though your heart is breaking"; "put on a happy face"; "you've made your bed, now sleep in it". You likely have other dictums that you've inherited from your elders. I guess they survived by doing it that way. I am inclined to call it denial. I have witnessed the devastating effects of such attitudes in my generation. In my family system, breakdown was regarded as a weakness - whether it was about "nervous breakdown", job loss, change, religious defection, marriage dissolution, changing national allegiance or worse yet, changing political parties! If you suffered breakdown in any of these areas you were considered INVALID. You were weak and were treated as AN INVALID.

There were few stories shared about one's breakdown. In fact, the victories were not to be celebrated too loudly either. Extremes were avoided at all cost. My grandfathers were both Alsatian and there was a definite sobriety that went along with that! To be raised without a mythology to support *an essential element of human existence* is hazardous for human living. The religious myths which had the information and energy to help us were *sterilized* to purify the humanity of God as seen in Jesus and his mother Mary. To have suggested them as models of human struggle and growth rather than as "above humanity" would have been very useful to my faith and my life in general. And to share personal story - especially among the males - was considered weak and disgusting. As a result, the survival tactics were kept from us and we continue on our merry way into adulthood with few tools for the inevitable stumbles.

There is a principle of physics that states that everything on this earth has both rise and fall, elation and depression. This law of the earth applies as well to the "earth creature" that we are. Depression is as *normal* as elation. IT IS PART OF THE PACKAGE. A people that cannot suffer cannot celebrate. You cannot have Easter without Lent. You cannot have life without death. We are a generation that has been bred to *deny* and as a result we have tried to satisfy ourselves with the PSEUDO. Simply look at our popular heros and you get a glimpse of what I mean (Marilyn Monroe, Michael Jackson, Madonna). As a result we are also content (?) with pseudo-food, pseudo-sex and pseudo-relationship without the intimacy that the REAL demands.

REAL hurts sometimes. PSEUDO tranquilizes. That is what results from the "poisonous pedagogy" that we have inherited from a generation that decided for their survival that *denial is better.* Alcohol, cigarettes and automobiles are part of what their disease has left us to deal with. Please God, let us model truth to the next generation!

Breakdown and depression are normal. It is where we are given the opportunity in our eco-system to GROW and embrace more profound and more expansive reality. To drug them away means to remove the opportunity that crisis offers us. Deciding how to get out of it, beyond it, through it is what creates the survival repertoire and the good human energy we need for the next passages we inevitably face. Without facing change we never grow to enjoy it. We learn to just *put up with it.*

We have great need for myths, models and methodology to aid us in the human journey. Elders in the human community are people who have worked long and hard at the "practice of survival". We need elders who can share their story with the next generation. We each need *someone* who can share his truth, show us the wounds and assure us that we can live through dilemma. It is an imperative for the continuation of the "human" race. This is much more imperative than economic survival! Yet the mythological gross national product seems to be the most important reality for this generation and its governments.

Loss of Soul:*burnout*

Chapter Three

Symptoms

Over the past years I have sat with hundreds of women and men and heard stories of their sadness and fears as they finally dealt with the devastating realities of soul loss. Indeed they had poor vocabulary to describe the ravages of burnout but as they began their litany I saw strong similarities emerging in the language they used. Often it was difficult for me to hear them since their confession echoed my own 1981 breakdown. Their articulation developed after several months of release. The first few sessions were generally times for tears, tissues and tenderness. The images, the symptoms emerged little by little. Often the feelings had been "nicely" frozen, denial reigned and even though there were breakthroughs, the well established facades would return as the urgency of healing subsided. What did it look like, this soul loss? Feel like?

The images that have emerged as this generation has bared its soul to me are countless.

The Litany

As I have crossed the country speaking to groups ranging from CEO's to nurses, from clergy to social workers, from managers to funeral directors, I have gathered words and images that describe what is going on when this soul-loss occurs. Check yourself out - -

I'm treading water.
I'm dancing as fast as I can.
I'm disappointed.
I feel like a gerbil on a treadmill.
I'm confused.
I live in despair.
I feel compressed.
I'm angry.
I'm totally spent. Nothing left!
I'm hyper-critical.
I'm overwhelmed.
I'm exhausted all over.
My name is FEAR!
I'm out of control.
I'm scattered.
I'm bitter.
I have brain over-load.
I feel betrayed.
I feel as though I'm trapped.
I feel alone and abandoned.
I feel guilty.
I want to crawl into a hole and pull the lid over it.
Just leave me alone!
I feel as though I'm being held together with masking tape.
I feel defeated.
I feel grey.
I feel drained.
I feel in conflict because I really shouldn't feel this way.
Sigh!!!!
I feel battered.
I am paralyzed.
I feel incompetent.
I've lost my light.
I don't want to be an adult anymore. I just want to be me.
I feel depressed.
I am always cranky.

I feel shitty.
I feel rejected.
I am mouldable and vulnerable.
I feel cold.
I am just dry bones.
I am in a meat grinder.
I am multiple. On a split screen.
I feel expendable.
I've had to stick my whole body (not just my finger) into the dike.
I am helpless.
The institution has nailed my feet to the cross and I'm not allowed to dance.
My feet are in cement.
I am always gasping for breath.
This is a boundaries' dance.
I feel useless.
I am ALWAYS driven. No energy.
I am sexually dead. I have no interest or energy for it.
I am reactive rather than responsive.
I feel physically ill. I've always got a cold or the flu. Can't shake it.
I'm out of character.
I feel different.
Of all the things I've lost, I miss my mind the most!
I feel public.
I'm losing it.
I can't find it!
I've withdrawn from living!
I feel claustrophobic.
I'm panic stricken.
I'm crying behind my eyes.
My body is a dangerous and bothersome territory.
I'm running on fumes.
I feel like I'm drinking from a waterfall.
Just hold me! I can't feel myself!
I'm sitting at the crossroads of expectation.
I live in a small space in my own body.
I live in my own "reserve".

The most difficult moment of any healing process is the long and arduous battle to find the appropriate words. It takes time, energy and sometimes assistance to get the correct words to identify what is really going on in one's pain. Often as I have worked with people I have been able to suggest a word. "That's it! How did you know?"

Perhaps the list will offer you words you have not had the imagination to find to describe your inner state. The therapist or the elder is simply someone who has the resources available from his storehouse of experience (and hopefully from his own story) to shed creative fresh light onto your story. Also the therapist or elder has the appropriate stories to stir up and reinforce your own story. You may be going crazy but that is the way we grow. I have and others have also. The therapist or elder can illustrate your condition through some archetypal myths that illustrate where you are now. It's ok. Painful. But ok.

Once the backdrop has been safely drawn one can proceed creatively to explore the inner geography of soul. However, true exploration for growth cannot take place until a backdrop is established that does not pathologize breakdown and crisis. Breakdown is normal. *Live* through it. IT IS NOT BAD!!! It is only tough!

It is difficult to isolate what happens when one begins to lose a sense of soul. However, a number of constants have been evident to me in my work with people who claim to be suffering from "burnout".

1. Tears

Humans experience different types of tears. We all experience the tears of hurt that come from a physical wound. These tears differ from tears of rage or tears of abandonment and differ yet from tears of grief from the loss of a loved one. Tears of joy and elation are still other. The tears that accompany soul-loss are tears for a *dead self*. They can take the form of outbursts in the silence of one's locked car or one's bedroom. They can explode embarrassingly in the middle of a boardroom meeting with colleagues. Or they can accompany one's life as a sad cello mourning in the background. They are often described as an inner well that emerges with every new request for help or with every phone ring. I had one client's tears spurt out onto *my* face as *she* erupted in sadness.

In my own saga, the tears began the morning of my breakdown. They continued for six months. Driving up the highway that morning, the inner sadness was too deep. The tears just erupted. They accompanied my days and nights as a whimpering child locked in his crib with the deep sense that momma had abandoned him. No way out. No way in. Just sad.

The deepest guilt over tears comes from the males. There is little acceptance for tears in the male. They are considered to be a sign of weakness. Crying is judged to be inappropriate and "feminine". How many males have cried for an entire session with me because they had held in the pain of a parent's or pet's death for forty years?

A few years ago, I was in a therapy session with my own therapist and three other males. We were working for an entire Saturday on "father" issues. I went to the session convinced that I would be working on unfinished business regarding my step-father. After a morning of breathing, stretching and guided imagery in order to loosen up our feelings, we began our "mat trips" where we work out our feelings in the midst of our colleagues. I went second after an explosive confrere vented which stirred up my own emotion. After two minutes I screamed out, "DON'T TAKE MY DADDY AWAY FROM ME!" The therapist asked me what I was seeing. "MY DADDY IS IN A CASKET AND THOSE MEN ARE TAKING HIM AWAY FROM ME!" was my reply. I sobbed and wailed for 45 minutes. In the bioenergetics session, the therapist had touched a point on my back that triggered memory. I HAD NEVER, IN 50 YEARS, GRIEVED THE DEATH OF LEONARD SCHUETT <u>OUT LOUD</u>!!! The men held me and let me cry. Thank God.

For 50 years I had been walking around with what turned out to be my *core grief* embedded in my psyche. My dad's leaving me was the source of my deepest sadness, grief and sense of abandonment. And yet Leonard Schuett had no desire to abandon me. He just died! The unexpressed sadness had lodged itself somewhere in my eco-system. It took a sensitive therapist to unmask it with precious touch. Sad energy does not just disappear. If you think it has, you will be surprised when suddenly it appears in the most unexpected places.

Remember:

SAD ENERGY THAT DOESN'T GET <u>EXPRESSED</u>
GETS <u>SUPPRESSED</u>
AND LEADS TO <u>DEPRESSION.</u>

Bill had been a bed wetter. "Billy peed his pants" was a tune he carried with him through his youth. He responded to the teasing with tears and rage. One morning his wife called me at 02:00 and asked me to visit their fashionable suburban home. She advised me that I would "have to see for myself" what had happened when I arrived. Everything in the house had been smashed! In a simple enough household dispute, she had called him "stupid". That triggered the bed wetting refrain and with it the same rage and tears that had accompanied "Billy" all his life. I found him cowering in the corner of the recreation room with his thumb in his mouth, his head between his legs, sobbing. I held him and we cried together. "She told me I was stupid," he sobbed.

That OLD FEELING re-emerges and overwhelms our present reality sometimes. The tears flow.

Peter came to see me with a true concern about tears. Now in his mid-40's he was experiencing loss of self. A very successful lawyer with a strong political career, a good and happy spouse and father, a much loved son and president of his dad's company. All of a sudden he was overcome with tears. They never left him. He was unable to be at work, embarrassed to be at home with his family and frightened to be by himself. The only place he felt safe was in my office where he dared confess to tears. Overwhelmed. Over-responsible. Too big too soon. Never a child. Always "responsible and in charge". At 45 the true child emerged. Sad. Lonely. Frightened.

Tears are one of the best barometers we have of knowing that we are in trouble. We can often deny our grief and cover up in order to manage life. But tears that have been suppressed for years will finally come out - as tears, if we are fortunate; as rage and destruction if we are not so lucky.

I asked my aunt if my grief had been handled after my dad's death. I was 2. She reminded me that I was pre-verbal and that my mom's grief was uppermost on everyone's mind as she was a young widow at 28. However, she did remember that for four months after my dad's death I acted out. Here's what happened:

Before Dad died, Mom would call him for dinner by banging on the stove-pipe that ran from our apartment down into the furniture store he owned. He would hear it and come up for the meal. For months after the funeral, I would bang on the pipe. He never came.

I returned to Mildmay, Ontario to the John F. Schuett and Sons furniture store a few months ago and in the old apartment discovered a stove-pipe with the hugest dent you'd ever want to see, about knee's height. Kelly had cried out. With a stick! It took 38 more years for the true tears to emerge and another ten for the truth to come out and healing to occur.

REMEMBER: HEALING TAKES TIME!

2. Slurrrrrrrrrrrr

Burnout can happen to anyone! Generally, however, people suffering from burnout have one or more of the following characteristics: they are over-generous, boundary-less, caring and/or perfectionists. Regardless, when there is no more energy to hold the pieces together the system falls apart. Simple. Slouches don't generally burn out. What is hard is that people who generally have been fastidious, dependable and committed, begin to show signs of *slipping*. Here are a few examples.

Monsignor was entertaining me in his living room after a preaching assignment in the South. He was a gentle Irish pastor with a heart as big as the moon and a sense of duty that was unequalled. In the few moments of leisure after lunch that Sunday afternoon, he sat back in his recliner - equipped for the fashionable celibate with a heater, a vibrator and a stereo system in the headrest - pulled out the tab of his Roman collar, began to say his breviary, watched the football game on

TV, listened to the baseball game on the headset, smoked his cigar and calmly spoke to me about the insincerity and laziness of the younger clergy. Amazing! That's slurrr - DOING EVERYTHING AND NOTHING AT THE SAME TIME!

Slurrr happens when you dial a phone number, let it ring and ask yourself, "Now, who am I calling?"

Slurrr happens when you have eighty things to do on your desk and can't begin or end anything.

Slurrr happens when you go to the basement to fetch something and upon your arrival wonder, "Why did I come down here?" It becomes more serious when you don't know <u>where</u> you are!

Slurrr happens when you get into the car and begin to drive in one direction and either wonder where you are going or realize that your destination was in the other direction. One funeral director once told me about a 200 car funeral which he had dutifully lined up to go in one direction to the cemetery only to realize that the cemetery was in the other direction in a busy downtown area.

Slurrr happens when you go to say one thing and another slips out. Or your tongue is too numb to be able to say complete words. Or your ideas slip. So many people in burnout forget important matters and double or triple book appointments.

People can forgive slurrr for a while. You even forgive yourself for a while. But after a few major errors, people are not amused. What at first looks like fatigue is often perilous. A surgeon client once related operating table stories. Frightening! And the health professionals are supposed to be models of the healing they profess. The most zombie-like people I have ever had to work with were medical residents and interns. They are being bred to be unhealthy. This is indeed dangerous. Think about it!

Slurrr is apparent to me when I cannot bear eye contact with another person. Every eye contact has three possible threats:

1. They will see that I'm "NOT THERE".
2. They will request something of me.
3. They will tell me how good I am. I DON'T BELIEVE THEM!

This is always a good indicator to me that I am in trouble. I love to have eye contact with people. When I am threatened by it, I know that I'm in deep trouble. Along with the tears, it is a good barometer for me as to whether I am in danger of once again falling into burnout mode. IF IT HAPPENED ONCE, IT CAN HAPPEN AGAIN! PAY ATTENTION TO YOUR BODY RESPONSES!

3. Internal Combustion

In any balanced ecological system, all the elements, which are intimately inter-connected and inter-related, are working in harmony with each other. When the source of energy is depleted or even weakened within a system, the parts fall out of harmony with each other and the system becomes dysfunctional. Little by little, the dischord sounds and breakdown occurs throughout the system.

Each of us is an eco-system within a larger eco-system. We are "earth creatures" and as such are in or out of harmony with ourselves and the earth where we dwell. The symptoms we are exploring here are what results from the lack of harmony that good health requires within our eco-system.

The expression UP TIGHT was forged in the 60's and 70's. It illustrates very well what is meant by burnout. In fact, in this condition, the whole eco-system is in a state of contraction. Were you to stand and contract every muscle from your toes to your head, you would get a good feeling for what you are like when you are in this traumatic state. What generally happens, however, is that you have been like this for so long, you no longer consider it abnormal. You forget what a pleasure the relaxed state was!

As a result of this acute tension, our entire being is in a state of inner pain. No part of a person can bear the brunt of this state forever. After some time the pain will begin to manifest itself. We begin to explode or implode on our own system. Then we combust in the other aspects of our life involving people, institutions and the environment. Our whole human eco-system has become unglued.

Gastro-intestinal eruption is one of the most obvious manifestations of this dis-ease. When antacids seem more vital to your health than food, you get a glimpse of the picture. Your stomach has to fight back with something when you rush and cram inappropriate substances down your gullet. In a time of deep distress we are more inclined to eat greasy foods, fats, sugar, caffeine and alcohol. Some of us will also be inclined to smoke, toke or sniff. Not good for the system. Acid is produced to scream out that something bad is going on. Rather than change what we ingest, we are more inclined to bandage with antacids or drugs.

A system that is struggling for freedom with an up-tight energy source is bound to experience pain in a variety of manners. Headache, backache, tooth decay, blurred vision, dizziness. So often clients have indicated to me that they feared they were having a heart attack because of the intensity of stabbing pain. Likely it was a systemic attack that was happening. How often people *have had* a heart attack or a stroke as a direct result of the prolonged agony of this condition. A BODY CAN ONLY TAKE SO MUCH. Then it gives out on us!

In my own journey of tears as I was in the throws of this disease, I suffered from severe bouts of nausea and diarrhea. They were indications to me that my self was throwing myself out. I was no longer able to contain myself and began to self-delete and unravel. These symptoms are common in this process of dying. Often they last for months and are only controlled once the soul has been recovered. Medication can help, but once again it is only a bandage or a bridge solution.

Earlier I spoke of breath-less-ness. Breath is the source of our being. The Ancients understood that when the breath was gone, the soul was gone. Clients have told me innumerable tales of hyper-ventilation, shallow breathing and fainting spells. They speak of exhaustion that can lead to depression or death. Once again, stimulation of breathing can break the grasp of depression.

No story of burnout is complete without mention of chronic fatigue. It is generally what people notice first about themselves. They talk about always being tired - never able to catch up on their rest. They talk about a fatigue that no sleep, no vacation, no drug could heal. The internal combustion of burnout is systemic exhaustion. Systemic relaxation is required to overcome it. I believe that the discussion around "chronic fatigue syndrome" is sometimes out of touch with the spiritual dimension of this disease. We are not talking about something that ultimately drugs or therapy sessions can cure (although they may be an integral part of the healing process). We are talking about spiritual grounding. Soul recovery. Deep recovery.

4. Withdrawal

When one is grounded within the universe, when one's eco-system is in balance and in harmony, it is possible to "be well" without external referents. It is possible to en-joy and to take pleasure and delight in "being". But when one's being is shaky, when one's validity or delight is defined almost completely by "other", it is probable that one is living in shame and guilt.

We are a generation that has been bred to have validity through the perfect drink, the correct designer label, the right house or car. We also have been conditioned - even through religion - to have validity only through being-for-others, by being self-less and self-effacing. It has been difficult for us as a civilization to have good self-worth, indigenous pride and honour. The Europeans brought this disease to this continent as the First Nations Peoples remind us. As a result of *this new world view* peoples have gone into deep shame and have had their souls ravaged by alcohol and drugs. No one was invalid, un-employed or useless in native societies. These peoples were linked to the worlds known to them - both the visible earthly world as well as the mystical dream and mythical world. They were at peace. We have invalidated the invisible and as a result have isolated and deified the seemingly "real" world. This is our problem!

So, living within the *visible, doing* world that we have considered *real*, contemporary humans suffer from isolation. As a result, when we are overwhelmed with work, caring, success etc., we become fearful and become paranoid because of our ungroundedness. Humans without roots, without undergirding begin to doubt their own being and begin to live with the overwhelming message that they have no value unless they are visibly successful within the context of "consumerism and business". Imagine giving yourself value based on Western *Civilization* and the *capitalist economy* of which we have become the pawns! As a result, contemporary humans live with a pall of fear that intimidates them and denies their *true* value. We must never forget that SYSTEMS ONLY HAVE VALUE BECAUSE OF US - NOT VICE VERSA!

The question of burnout cannot be understood outside this context. For it has arisen as a human epidemic within the context of THIS civilization and not until NOW.

The people who have come to me speak of paranoia, fear, depression, loneliness, bitterness, sadness, cynicism, boredom and withdrawal. These are not "slight" people. They are generally the very good, very productive types and honoured among people. But they have lost it! And more often than not, it has been in *doing it*. They have become the victims of the needs of this society and their own insatiable need to please and help. Depleted of inner energy they begin to find themselves retreating from the normal activity that defined them and gave them value. They begin to see themselves as spotted, illegitimate, unworthy, stupid, flawed. More often than not, they are not so perceived by their peers. On the contrary. But as their own self worth diminishes, their systems shut down. Eventually (and this they fear deeply) their peers begin to "catch on" as well.

5. Explosion

Rage is a bigger word than most people would use to talk about inner anger but my experience with these *very good, very appropriate, very nice* people is just that. They are filled with rage - rage that is unexpressed (as that would break the image); rage that has been held in (and turned onto self rather than at the appropriate targets); rage that has been denied (because *I'm afraid of it and besides, I don't even know how to DO it!*).

Rage takes many forms.

It can take the form of immediate explosion. This often surprises the overly caring sort of person because it is so rare an event for them. What is frightening is when it happens more often, more easily and in a more public manner. Because this is also inappropriate in most settings, the added factor of guilt is present. How can I do something like that? We are generally unaware of the intensity of the rage that dwells under the skin of the "really and truly *good*". Often the goodness is the result of control and denial that has been bred in us - or passed along as the "Christian way to be". We have forgotten that Jesus let his rage rip on a few occasions - and *very inappropriately* as far as his family and rabbis would have been concerned.

I find the more religiously repressed a person is, the more deep seated is their rage. I am amazed at the rage that the Christian fundamentalist preachers (and the Moslem, Jewish and other fundamentalist preachers) expose as they vent on the tube! The rallies of the righteous are very frightening things to behold! Their energy is shame-based rather than grounded on love and delight.

Rage often shows its face in the form of substance abuse. It is generally a rage thrown back on self, but truly is as well a slap in the face of the universe. Whether it be food, alcohol, nicotine or drugs, the slow suicide that ensues is the silent (and often not too silent) cry of rage. A person with a strong belief in self, with a soul in harmony with the universe has no need to disappear. And this is exactly what happens with substance abuse. I MAKE MYSELF INVISIBLE (I think!). This rage also embraces everyone who is involved with the person as it is dependent on everyone else maintaining the lie that the emperor has clothes. The addict always enslaves a certain number of followers with correspondingly weak soul-energy. This is as true with the work addict or the boundary-less caregiver. What masquerades as jolly, open, kind and stretching is often really egocentric, insecure and narcissistic.

Rage also, at times, will take the form of avoidance. It sometimes takes the form of sexual dysfunction or lack of interest, or in the flight from true intimacy. Sometimes, on the other hand it will take the shape of sexual promiscuity or obsession. It is pleasure mixed with deep sadness and tears. (See Ann Wilson Schaef, ESCAPE FROM INTIMACY.)

Marion Woodman claims that the opposite of love is not hatred but CONTROL. Control, I believe, is another form of rage. Someone with a contented soul has no need to control anyone. Everyone's being is valid and has a place in the universe. But insecurity breeds control. And control breeds more control. Hand in hand with this expression of rage is perfectionism. With this disorder, I need not only control myself but another as well. Nothing is ever perfect, so more and more control is needed to ensure the quality of the product whether that product be the business, you or me. The addict makes himself as a god (and so often with a *humble* facade). In religious circles I have met more arrogant people who pose as humble. Just try to bend them! It is their way or the highway. But then, you know, that with the highway there is no salvation! Who says?

The final expression of rage that I also have been partner to in my own story as well as in hundreds of others' is suicide. Besides the illusion that it is the only "way out" it also promotes the illusion that this act will put all at peace. In the end it is the ultimate act of ego-centricity as it places one's being at the core of everything. The victim of this illusion becomes blinded to the devastating effects of the act on family, friends and colleagues. Yet it is a most understandable aspect of depression and a form that most of us have known at one point of our life or another.

Marion Woodman says it better than anyone.

Many people can listen to their cat more intelligently than they can listen to their despised body. Because they attend to their pet in a cherishing way, it returns their love. Their body, however, may have let out an earth shattering scream in order to be heard at all. Before symptoms manifest, quieter screams appear in dreams: a forsaken baby elephant, a starving kitten, a dog with a leg ripped out. Almost always the wounded animal is either gently attempting to attract the attention of the dreamer, who may or may not respond...

It is possible that the scream that comes from the forsaken body, the scream that manifests in a symptom, is a cry of the soul that can find no other way to be heard. If we have lived behind a mask all our lives, sooner or later - if we are lucky - the mask will be smashed. Then we will have to look in our mirror at our own reality. Perhaps we will be appalled. Perhaps we will look into the terrified eyes of our own tiny child, that child who has never known love and who now beseeches us to respond. This child is alone, forsaken before we left the womb, or at birth, or when we began to please our parents and learned to put on our best performance in order to be accepted. As life progresses, we may continue to abandon our child by pleasing others - teachers, professors, bosses, friends and partners, even analysts. The child who is our very soul cries out from under the rubble of our lives, often from the core of our worst complex, begging us to say, "You are not alone. I love you." from THE PREGNANT VIRGIN

Loss of Soul:*burnout*

Chapter Four

Roots

Where does this boundary-less, driving need to DO RELENTLESS-LY come from? In my early years I thought that it came from a person's desire to succeed or from an inner sense of small worth. I also thought that it was passion run amuck. All that would be needed to help the person re-balance was to help him modify his behaviour. So - breathing, stretching and aerobic programmes, time management programmes, nutritional guidance, relationship counselling.

As I worked with individual after individual, I began to realize that this was a fine approach on one level, only it failed to get at the heart of the matter. What I often found, however, was that the individual simply transfered the disorder from work to "getting fit", from caring to food, from perfectionism to religion.

It was while doing work at a prison that I began to see substance addicts become impassioned by religion and take it on as a fresh addictive substance. They began to "terrorize" the inmates as well as the chaplains as they tried to push their new drug on everyone.

It was in this process of transfer that I began to realize that the successful, refined, nice people who generally came to me for burnout recovery were addicts as well. Their substance was simply desired, sup-

41

ported, given accolade and rewarded by sick organizations from the business firm to the church to the family. Sickness with great rewards.

When one dentist announced that for her recovery she would have to abandon her practice, her greatest opponents were her children who pleaded with her not to do so because *their identity was in question* due to her decision. Their systems required her disease! So it was with my decision to leave the practice of ministry in the Catholic Church. There were great rewards for being sick - adulation, gifts, prestige and pseudo-belonging. The disapproval and shunning which results from *telling the truth* in religious organization is overwhelming. Recovery is not respected. Breakdown is looked upon as disease and one is generally treated as an embarrassment to the leadership. So cover-up and denial reign!

It was through the experience with my burnout clients that I began to realize that the only way to their true healing was to treat them as I would treat an addict. At least, it is the only approach that I have experienced that WORKS! What I am illustrating in the following pages is what worked for me and my clientele. There are, I hope, other approaches that will truly help people recover.

Ninety percent of the people who have come to me over the years for burnout counselling have been either first born children or babies in the family. Most of them have *put on* a compliance script. They attempted to live out the dreams, expectations, hopes and fears of their primary caregivers. This could be their parents, grandparents, mythological figures, God, teachers, clergy, therapists - anyone to whom they felt they should be accountable. It is interesting that as I tour North America giving lectures on this topic, a huge number of participants (generally from education, health care, funeral services, social work, clergy) are first born or babies.

Many people choose their life career out of a "pleasing parent" syndrome. They makes their choices out of inner sadness and shame. I have lived with many priests whose mother had the vocation to the priesthood - not them. I knew one man who left the priesthood and married the week after the death of his mother!

Many children are bred to be the one responsible for the rest of the family. Often they become the surrogate husband or wife in a dysfunctional relationship between mother and father. Often they are given the heavy burden of living out the unfulfilled dreams of either parent. In the case of immigrant children or children of refugees or ex-concentration camp prisoners similar scripts are handed down. The clients I have had the most difficulty with in the recovery process have been children of religious zealots. Their very soul (with its imagination and feelings) has been captured. They are often immobilized in living their lives before the ominous Judge (God) as well as before the very visible judges (their family or the religious comunity).

Nearly all the clients I have seen over the past years have come out of some form of sadness in their family of origin - either abuse or addiction. Sometimes it has been very difficult for them to name the source of sadness or of "wipe-out" as they have not considered work or caring or religion or perfectionism to be addiction. Often the family dysfunction was masked by wealth, propriety or piety. Within that context, everything *looked* fine. But secretly, inside everything *felt* awful. Sometimes it was a parent's "success drive" that killed their soul. Especially in upper-class where the successful business man used his family as part of his "excellence stratagem", the wife, children - even the pets - have to *match* his inner image of success. How difficult it has been working with the adult children of this *perfect* picture.

In one family I worked with, the father in the family had purchased a very large, expensive picture frame for his office within which to expose his family. His children sabotaged his dream by not allowing themselves to be photographed with him. They told him that there was no *family* and so a family portrait was out of the question. He had been so absent from the family for years that they no longer considered him part of the family. How painful the truth coming from children can be. Later, the wife and children divorced the husband. His true family was his work. I hope he gets the picture!

The addiction literature has been very helpful over the past few years in giving us insights into the roots of the process that leads to soul loss. The *child* is another word to talk about the *self* or the *soul*. Other cultures speak of the radiant child, the divine child, the golden child, the inner child. Each of us has some sense of who that *truest me* looks and feels like. It is as though there was some innate knowledge of what I *really* am. Then there is the *pseudo-self,* the mask or masks that I have had to put on for survival or acceptance. There are pseudo-feelings, denied or frozen and at the core of my being is the truth that persists despite the cover-up that I have had to maintain in order to make it through the days and nights.

It is very important that in these discussions about loss of child - of soul, of self - we do not ascribe guilt to ourselves. Most of us have survived long enough to read this book due to the fact that we were crafty. We likely did *put on* behaviour for survival but we have survived. At mid-life most of us yearn for truth. So then, or now as the case may be, we re-cover our true self. Or, more often than not, we DIS-COVER or UN-COVER our true selves, our souls. That is ok. Many have died who didn't. You are doing it and you are alive!

I often beat myself up when I realize that at 15 years of age I entered the Christian Brothers. I left one dysfunctional family and sought another. At the age of 15, I wore a black robe with a little white collar and a scull cap. I took on the name *Brother Patrick* and for two years led a life of denial and penance. I was 15! What was considered *normal* and *heroic* for an Irish-Catholic kid I would now consider abusive and sick. But that was then and this is now. One of my psychiatrist colleagues reminded me a while back that I was a crafty kid and smart enough to find an acceptable way of breaking forth from my own dysfunctional family and to claim my own life <u>AT 15</u>!!! It was a crazy place to be. The spirituality was gnostic and unhealthy. Some of the men were deviant. Others, however were the best friends a kid could ever want. BUT I CLAIMED MY LIFE AND BROKE AWAY FROM DISEASE by leaving home again!!!

Within a year my eco-system began its work. I began to suffer from mononucleosis and anorexia nervosa and was hospitalized. MY SOUL PUSHED MY WHOLE ECO-SYSTEM INTO SPASM! And my body began to tell me, "No you don't! Save yourself! Get out of here! THIS IS NOT YOU!!!" It took me a year or so to listen to myself that time. Once again KELLY emerged. Old in many ways (I had renounced my child at 15) but new again. I lived the next few years feeling like an "ex-con". I was an embarrassment to my step-father, a worry for my mother and questionable in the eyes of the Irish-Catholic parish where I grew up. I forgot that I was one of hundreds in the same situation. Just one more victim! I felt like a failure. Now I realize I had also gained a great deal of wisdom for a 15 year old - wisdom that would serve me for the rest of my life.

How sad it is to see little children in primary grades who have renounced *their child* in honour of tyrants and addictive people and systems. Their eyes are sad. Their bodies already bear the marks of heavy responsibility and powerlessness. It is Alice Miller, I believe, who has the best grasp on the subject of "the child". In FOR YOUR OWN GOOD, (Hidden Cruelty in Childhood and the Roots of Violence), she speaks of the "poisonous pedagogy" that goes on in dysfunctional family systems where the child is victim of the adult's crazy thinking and behaviour. With deep feelings of abandonment, the child begins to internalize a script of unworthiness, feelings of being wrong, flawed, useless. This often flows from family or child rearing scripts that have been passed on without question from one generation to another, often in the name of God.

Addiction literature speaks about the "shame" that one experiences and feels as a result of abandonment. This concept has been captivating in my understanding of what pushes otherwise sane and delightful people over the edge in their generosity-with-self-unto-death. It begins with a primary sense of being *wrong, flawed, a mistake, awful, a fraud - uworthy*. It is salved by a "mask" of perfection, of flawlessness, of smiling openness, of availability.

Shame arises in a person when he feels that some significant other walks away. That *feeling* has nothing to do with the absent one necessarily. I *felt* that my dad abandoned me. I was angry, in deep pain and *felt* abandoned. Leonard Schuett did not abandon me. He just died! When the physician parent is never home for a meal, always absent from the ball game, the child goes into a state of inner *wipe out* that after awhile inscribes itself onto his soul. Initially it was just a bruise. Little by little it becomes indelible. It takes over and eventually, unless there are counteractive positive strokes, his soul *becomes* shame.

The shame grows as there is more and more evidence that one is surely "no damn good" at all. Once the soul is convinced that it is flawed, everything else just latches on like a zebra mussel.

I have *twin toes*. There is nothing wrong with that. As a little boy my mother told me that having twin toes was a lucky sign. It meant that I would travel across the seas. It was a good message from her. In fact, I have been across the seas hundreds of times (on a plane). My step-father, however, told me that I had "monkey feet". Guess who I believed?

A few years ago I was walking along the beach north of Playa del Carmen in Mexico. It was at the end of a fabulous vacation. The sun was at its best, the sand and water were superb. I was blessing the Creator for the great gift. Suddenly my eyes caught sight of a man swimming with his son on his back. My step-dad did that with me. I started to cry. I looked at my feet and cried out, "He said I had monkey feet." And I lost it.

But then, from somewhere truer within me came the message, "That is not true. It was an unfair thing to say to you. You interpreted that your whole being was flawed because he put you down again in his bully-ish way. YOU ARE FINE. YOUR FEET ARE FINE. THEY HAVE CARRIED YOU FOR 48 YEARS AND THEY AND YOU ARE FINE!!!!" I exclaimed OUT LOUD. I picked up a shell and a piece of coral as I said it and touched my feet. I took the "memory clicks" back to Toronto with me and put them in front of a little shrine with a picture of myself at 3 years of age. I return to it regularly to remind myself that I am not flawed, that I am a gracious, lovely creature and worthy.

It is amazing how we get *old messages* that are triggered by new people in our lives. "When I look at you, I get that old feeling," the song goes. Marilyn Mason calls them "internal hemorrhages". John Bradshaw calls them "shame spirals". The point is clear. New events can sometimes trigger old feelings that have been embedded into our eco-systems. The fuse just has to be hinted at and off we go into the same psycho-space as in the past. Feelings, images, smells and events are re-experienced. Remember "Billy peed his pants"?

In beginning times of shame, we are inclined to rub things off to minimize these messages. That is ok. As time progresses and the shaming continues, we learn to build survival mechanisms. They become our silent friends. Sometimes they take the shape of a smile, or showing that we care, or "looking after" everybody, or eating, or doing. The list is long. We put on behaviour that will ease the pain of our CORE GRIEF.

Most of us are survivors. We create mechanisms or behaviours to counterbalance the wound which has bred shame in us, a deep inner sense that we are really no good. We are amazing beings! What began as a valid and helpful crutch, eventually develops into a compulsion as the inner wipe-out continues. Every time the shame is experienced we return to the behaviour that boosted us up out of the despair. After several years of this, the action becomes automatic and we enter into the danger zone of addiction.

An addiction is an old friend that doesn't work anymore.

Once it becomes impossible to give up some behaviour, we can say that one is addicted. In the process for survival that we create out of inner grief, patterns of behaviour emerge that begin to strangle us. What was a friend becomes daemon. Rollo May gives us insight into this important area of reflection:

> The daimonic is any natural function which has the power to take over the whole person. Sex and eros, anger and rage, and the craving for power are examples. The daimonic can be either creative or destructive and is normally both. When this power goes awry and one element usurps control over the total personality, we have "daimon possession," the traditional name through history for psychosis...

> The daimonic is the urge in every being to affirm itself, assert itself, perpetuate and increase itself. The daimonic becomes evil when it usurps the total self *without regard to the integration of that self, or to the unique forms and desires of others and their need for integration.* (italics mine)

> Rollo May, LOVE AND WILL

Little by little, what began as a survival mechanism takes over. Behaviour which is good in itself becomes overwhelming to the point of putting a new face on the person. Thus one begins to speak of John as an "alcoholic", a "worry wart", a "shopaholic", a "workaholic". This is beyond using the term as an adjective but rather as an identity.

Burnout is present when *one's compulsions are so dominant that the self seems to disappear.* It is much more serious than simply being exhausted. It is about losing one's inner core to behaviour that brings on wipe-out. As a result of this inner exhaustion, the whole eco-system begins to collapse. When we talk of burnout we talk of a state of *systemic exhaustion.* There is no energy left to hold the parts together and the self *dis*-integrates.

This spills over into the lives of our families and colleagues as well. Unfortunately there is generally dis-integration of the relationships before healing takes place. This is a most devastating reality of this condition because the people who are closest to us are the ones who have the goods to help us heal. But after years of seeing us in *denial,* they often have no energy left for us as the burnout victim and have to walk away for their own survival.

Loss of Soul: *burnout*

Chapter Five

Choose Life

The greatest possible gift of any breakdown is that of rebirth. Jung speaks of the positive purposes of neurosis. In ancient mythologies as embodied in the religious *praxis* of various peoples, resurrection only comes after death, new identity after *tardemah*. Carnival, Lent and Easter are intimately linked in the Christian traditions. We plunge to depths in order to rise with new life. We *put on* the mysteries of life's ups and downs in costume, ritual, words, chant. One of the problems for the contemporary Western person is the utter absence of supporting rituals for the peaks and pits that life brings us. As a result we tend to be "out of practice" when our normal breakdowns occur. Breakdown is seen as "abnormal" in our contemporary worldview. Whenever or however we break down, it is seen as bad or wrong. We go into deepest denial with the ultimate "breakdown" - death. As the kids today say, "Shit happens", and when it does we have three alternatives.

The first one is to die. That is perhaps the easiest as we are not good at being overwhelmed. Many suicide - quickly or slowly. Many of us dig our own graves with a fork. Others with a bottle, drugs, or some other addictive behaviour. Some enter into "accidents" that are too obviously planned. Some insist on dysfunctional, sad relationships and die through despair.

Loss of Soul:*burnout*

Some decide to remain *undead - neither dead nor alive.* These are the people who refuse to engage with their breath, with the ground, with their intimates. They continue on as though there were no problem. Zombies, dulled of feeling, apathetic, bored. They often remain in key posts in some of our institutions and pass their disease on down through the ranks. They become health hazards and sad to look at. But often they are able to maintain the *mechanics* of the job and are well known as *important* and are therefore untouchable.

Others decide to live. And this alternative takes courage as it requires one to deal with breakdown. It often begins with a whimper. Some are prepared for breakdown and have appropriate life-support systems at hand. Others have just rehearsed all their lives for the moment of truth. Regardless, I hope this is the option you choose if you are in the midst of burnout. Reading these pages is a good first step.

Core Grief

The first moment of recovery is the hardest. To pass from denial to decision is difficult for many. To pass from knowledge to acknowledgement is terrifying for some people. But in order for true healing to take place one's *core grief* must be discerned, named and claimed. It is this long and often arduous adventure of naming the source of one's pain that frightens many people. Years of cover-up have sometimes buried deeply in the subconscious the memories and events related to one's core grief. It often takes a *variety* of therapeutic approaches to help one get at the root of pain that is deep enough to cause life-long static. Often we try to protect the parent or person who might have been at the source of our pain - even long after they are dead or out of the picture. Many sabotage their own healing and happy survival in this way. Many have difficulty saying words OUT LOUD to describe their core grief although their dreams are rampant with images and scenes. Often, also, a secondary event might be mistaken for the primary event or person who was at the source of the grief. I firmly believe that there is generally **one** major grief from which all others flow. As in exorcism, it is imperative to get the devil's *correct* name. Not just any name will grab the attention of the demon.

There have been many approaches to healing in this manner. Gershen Kaufman's book, SHAME is the best source I know of for healing the core grief out of which shame emerges. I know that recovery from toxic shame which the wounded child experiences is best done with assistance. John Bradshaw and Charles Whitfield offer excellent resource materials to help people probe into their own story. But I believe firmly from my experience that it is necessary to tell one's whole truth to <u>some</u> <u>other</u> <u>person</u> <u>or</u> <u>persons.</u> And this, several times. It takes time to believe oneself that the truth has finally been revealed. It also takes the sensitive care of a loving elder or therapist to truly listen and carry the weight of the story and feed it back. I have witnessed hundreds of incidents of overwhelming relief when the truth has finally been proclaimed. It is the OUT LOUD part that is important in healing. That there be another person to act as the *receiver* - one who can <u>echo</u> self acknowledgment - is a vital part of this dance.

Finding A Healer

I am not convinced that just anyone who is a therapist (psychiatrist, psychologist, social worker, counsellor) is able to do this kind of recovery work. In order to help *restore* soul, the healer must *have some.* I have witnessed too many people after years of psychiatric intervention at last discover someone, perhaps a non-professional who had the *gift* and enough human understanding to be able to lead through this very difficult work of recovery. I believe that an important gift of the healer is to LISTEN, to CARE and to BE ABLE TO <u>GO</u> <u>INTO</u> THE DARK, DESPERATE PLACES. Someone who has never been there is very often frightened or stand-offish. I am convinced that the healer must also possess, as part of his life repertoire, stories, myths and symbols to support the process. Recovery from loss of soul is major life passage work and needs a very *skilled mid-wife/elder/healer.* It is important that the person going through this process of recovery have the courage to interview people who can lead them through the work. It is also appropriate to change therapists if the person you have engaged does not have *what you feel you need* to get into your hidden places. Find another. Remember: THIS IS YOUR LIFE.

Loss of Soul: *burnout*

Jean Houston offers us this same wisdom when she says:

The violation of the natural weakness and simplicity of the young child not ready for autonomy can turn into a protective infantilism that lasts through one's life. The wounds may be redeemed through the natural simplicity of loving; indeed they may offer the gateway through which love may enter.

The Sacred Wound

This ancient Christian concept is of universal importance in the mystery of our breakdowns and recovery. We are all wounded. The sources of our pain are varied. The ways of healing are as varied as they need to be. Meister Johannes Eckhart, the 14th century Dominican mystic says that the best way for someone to pray is the way that's best for someone to pray. So too for healing the wounds that bind us. Whatever works for you is the best way for you to be healed. Whoever is the best healer for you is the best healer for you.

Another Dominican mystic, Catherine of Siena says that we were all created differently so we would all need each other. Why not? Ancient wisdom makes sense at any time of history. There have not always been psychiatrists and we have not always been crazy. The sources of healing exist within the planet for our survival - both physical and spiritual. We have canonized the "medical" and forgotten that *healing* exists in many places - even among the *broken down*. The sacralization of the medieval guilds is at long last showing its seams. Lawyers do not possess justice, the clergy do not possess spirituality and the physicians do not possess health. They all have access to it. So does every earth creature.

Our wounds, our inner grief, our breakdowns come out of our individual stories. No one is without them. We can all be healed from them. But we cannot deny them. They exist. And our story exists WITH them. They are both our death but also can be our redemption. It is also *because of them* that we have become who we are.

We create mechanisms for survival early in life that ease the pain of our wounds. Perhaps that energy has *taken over* in us and we have become crazy with caring, resolving, worrying, praying, working etc.

BUT we also have become *wonderful* in many ways as a result. We have had to stretch, be creative, crafty and resilient. We are not just messes. We are *gracious and blessed* messes!

What is devastating in the dance of survival is the *pain* at the source. That is what must be worked on. Most of us have excelled in living. Most of us wounded ones have been winners a hundredfold. But we have excelled *out of pain* and not out of radiance. We can finish the race. Inner transformation can change our sackcloth into dancing!

That deep transformation requires *changing the energy at the core*. In order to do that, we need the guidance of a healer to walk though the pain with us and to help us claim our own soul. It is necessary that we remove ourselves from the power of the wounder and claim our own power. That takes tears, telling and tackling of the enemy who has captured our energy for too long. This is the struggle that Jesus of Nazareth went through, John of the Cross in his dark night, Teresa of Avila in her years of spiritual aridity, that each human who has been free has struggled with. We do not deny the pain. We *go through it and claim it as positive energy for self and for the world*. We have been taught to deny pain, to deny sadness, to stuff feelings. Whereas to claim them as ours could be our tool for freedom. Sad energy is energy. It just needs to be transformed.

Many healers do their work out of sadness rather than radiance. I have taught in several divinity schools and have noticed that many who come to be prepared for ministry come with unresolved shame-issues. That is likely what pushes them into a ministry geared towards helping others. And that is fine. But often they do not bother with their own healing. As a result they begin with lots of energy but little by little they become toxic in their work with people and ultimately burn out (if they don't die first). Slow death is rampant among the healers of our land - either through alcohol and drugs (even prescribed ones) or food addiction. The rate of suicide is high among those in ministry as well.

The "wounded healer" is a valid concept but only if the healer has taken the plunge into resurrection. The post-resurrection Jesus came back and *exposed his wounds.* That is how they knew that he was the healer! Healers do not have to hide their wounds. When the wounds are integrated and assumed, they then possess terrific healing energy for others. What healers need to discover is that they do not have the right energy for everyone. That is why there are many of us. No one is everything to everyone. In burnout mode, some healers think that they can actually be all things to everyone.

What hitherto had been seen as weakness and a flaw, is just that. And weakness can be transformed into strength. The concluding chapter suggests some tools to transform such weakness, to recover one's truest self; one's lost soul; to recover **you.**

Loss of Soul:*burnout*

Chapter Six

Awakenings Without End

The *decision for life* is the most important part of the recovery process. That decision needs support on a variety of levels if one is to be able to stay on the path of life and not fall back into destructive behaviour rooted in shame. The process that leads to full, energetic, inter-dependent and generous life needs to be *embraced* and *practiced*.

We are an eco-system of energy. Every part of us is connected intimately to every part of us. We cannot "break down" in one area without affecting another part of the system. Fortunately or unfortunately, our eco-system surpasses our own physical realm and affects others and the energy of the earth as well. This planet will heal to the extent that you and I are willing to heal.

In burnout mode we generally forget that we are "earth creatures". Many of us have lived a perilous journey of self abuse coming from feeling like nobody and acting as though the whole universe depended on us. A major aspect of recovery is simply beginning to live *within our limitations* - respecting our nature which needs to be cared for.

The following comments outline the elements I believe are necessary for one to experience recovery. These elements flow out of practical wisdom gained through my own recovery as well as wisdom gained in helping others in the process.

1. Embrace Your Body

As tied up in *body* as contemporary Westerners seem to be, we are likely the least grounded society that has existed. We are definitely one of the least sexual although our pornographic quotient is the highest. Pseudo is the best word to describe a society that has had a hard time living with pain or pleasure.

Take time with your body. Body is not an addendum to who you are. IT IS YOU! Clear away some time for a date with your own body. Fill up the tub with hot water and bubble bath and just soak and shut up. Make the environment pleasant enough for a celebration of your body-existence. It is not wrong to take pleasure in your own body. We hurry about to the point of *living outside* ourselves. We fail to remember and to re-member ourselves. In the process of giving ourselves away, we forget our own exhausted selves. To JUST BE is likely the most difficult thing for us to do, despite the fact that we moan about not having time for our selves. When we do get such time, we are hesitant to use it for our selves. The body is the most obvious part of us. So it is a smart place to begin. Scents, candles, music can also help us *celebrate* our bodies in a healthy way.

It always fascinated me to know that the early Christians baptized their neophytes in cool running water, naked. Then they anointed them with *chrism*, an oil made of fragrant herbs. Early texts proclaim that the neophytes were to be anointed "from the top of their heads, to the bottom of their toes". They then were clothed in white garments and embraced by the rest of the community who lived "in the odour of sanctity". How strange, that such a community would, by the 20th century, have covered up their holy ones in black cloth from their heads to their toes with little radiance showing anywhere! It is ours to reclaim on the eve of the third millennium.

After the bathing, take some towels, dry yourself off and then begin a process of anointing and reclaiming. Start with your toes and work your way up. Speak to each part of yourself. Thank it for its fidelity to you over the years. I believe this kind of reclaiming will keep our body-system from crying out against us in disease. I also believe that it will introduce us to healthy pleasure; pleasure out of radiance rather than closet pleasure which comes out of shame.

2. Eat Well

Not lots. Well. Nourishingly. Eat chocolate, butter, chips and red meat. Drink coffee and alcohol. But only as a condiment or as a treat! None of these foods will kill most of us. However, when we go into depression, these are the foods we go after. And rather than lift us up as we believe they will (and do, for a brief moment), they depress us. We must begin to eat more nourishing foods.

Fat is an issue. No more than 25 percent of our calories - maximum! - should be fat. Saturated fat as in meat, butter, cream and other animal products should be limited to 7 percent of our calories. In North America fat constitutes the bulk of our diet. Check every day to test this out. If this is so, your body is having a hard time.

It would be best to eat like an Italian. The main meal should be at mid-day. That's almost impossible for most of us. But it can be done in terms of quantity of food. It would look something like this: a small serving of pasta; 85 grams of meat or fish (the size of a deck of playing cards), leafy greens or cruciferous vegetables (cabbage, broccoli, cauliflower); salad with oil and vinegar or lemon; fruit. The evening meal would be lighter. And no snack food during the evening!!! Let your body sleep in rest; not in the work of digesting food!

We should also keep weight in perspective. Our body types are all different. Our metabolisms are different. We inherit different body traits. We cannot all look the same. We are not all thin. For some of us, thin is not who we are. But we should avoid excess weight around the waist. That is more dangerous than hips or thighs.

Eating should not become an obsession. There should be pleasure attached to it as well. To eat with a note-pad is unnecessary. Just think and plan your diet so that there are conscious treats now and again. The Toronto dietician and chef Bonnie Stern always says that you should only eat dessert if it is scrumptious. Enjoy it. But don't waste your self on junk.

3. Sleep

Sleep because you have to. Sleep because you are tired. Sleep when your body calls out for it. Don't be afraid to nap. Not power nap. Just nap - daily if you can or need to. Find places to do it. In the car at lunch. At your desk. After work before dinner. On the weekend. Whenever. Beware, however, of sleeping too much as this can be avoidance of dealing with depression or burnout and for some a way of hiding.

Sleep also, to dream. Much soul recovery comes about in your sleep. Nature has endowed us with incredible recuperating devices. They are there for us to use. Conflicts are resolved, bliss is achieved, the un-imaginable becomes possible and balancing is done in our dream life.

There are also important messages about our future opened up to us in our sleep. To deny the possibility of this is to deny our soul. We are the first (so called) civilization to put so little weight on our dreams. We live as though the conscious were real and the sub-conscious unreal. Who says that one is any more real than the other? Are they not two aspects of our being? Why deny one in honour of the other? Respect for the sub-conscious will enhance the conscious aspect of our living.

4. Play

Do you have a playmate? Women seem to be better than men at investing time and energy on someone who is not their partner. Men seem to isolate after their 20's. Play is activity that has no particular end other than *being*. Many confuse games with play. Games can be play but often take on characteristics of competition, drivenness and perfectionism. If you are in burnout mode, it is especially important not to confuse these two things. Squashaholism is different from just *playing* squash.

Play also involves humour.

5. Laugh

Some have called humour *soul massage*. I try to start the day looking into the mirror and making myself laugh. It generally starts out contrived but within a few seconds it begins to *happen*. It makes me aware of an aspect of my being that is often left dormant as I am very stern like my Alsatian grandfathers. HUMOUR TAKES PRACTICE as does any human power! Humour also alters our breathing and helps us lighten up systemically. If I have a *serious* task to do, I put on a funny CD or film and it energizes me and prepares me for the job. Don't forget, *umor* means fluid, water. It is able to break down barriers and to turn granite into sand!

Humour that comes from inner radiance is positive and life-affirming. Humour that comes out of wound is cynical and sarcastic. Many people "cover up" their pain with humour. Certainly this is very characteristic of most of our contemporary TV humour. We are not happy campers as a society and our humour is a good barometer of the shame that binds our common soul.

Humour can lighten up serious tasks, create new connections with people, overcome barriers - even linguistic ones - and create hope. It entertains (*from the French entre-tenir - to hold together*) and binds us together in community. It is a way of seeing, salving and solving the serious issues of our lives if we give it a chance. It is grace under pressure and allows us to be creative in difficult times by introducing fun rather than seriousness into our dilemmas.

On my way to give a talk on humour in the workplace one winter day, Frank Milord, a Winnipeg taxi driver (also philosopher) told me the following: PROGRESS ONLY HAPPENS WHEN LAUGHTER IS VICTORIOUS OVER DOGMA. That's wisdom!

6. Breathe

Anything that can stimulate breathing is vital. People who generally breathe shallowly become depressed. Alexander Lowen says that the grasp of a depression can be loosened by deep and serious breathing. Every time I pick up his book, **DEPRESSION AND THE BODY**, I want to read and re-read it as he has understood so well the effects of breathing and stretching to re-stimulate hope in a depressed system.

Psychiatric therapy was a very important aspect of my own post-burnout healing but if it had not been supported by shiatsu therapy and acupuncture, my healing would only have been intellectual.

We should never forget that one never has just a *mental* breakdown. Access to the soul wound is possible from a variety of entry points. As the body remembers, it is a capital entry-point for healing. Shiatsu touches all the body-memory points and often a touch will trigger memory and allow tears and screams to flow that had been suppressed. WORDS ARE NOT OUR *ONLY* LANGUAGE AND OFTEN NOT OUR MOST HONEST.

Shiatsu, acupuncture and other body therapies and even the simple act of touch, stimulate blood flow, bring oxygen to the system and loosen the tight weave in the fabric of our lives. Such touch helps us to breathe - to breathe soul back into our lives.

I often suggest that people access their sadness by groaning. They generally begin with *head* sounds. I try to get them to move their grumble from their *head to their bowels*. It is *down there* that the core of their pain lodges. It is important that the sound travel through all the chakras as the pain is lodged *throughout* our body-system. We sometimes have major blockages in the heart, stomach and bowels. I believe this accounts for a lot of our contemporary disease in these areas.

7. Stretch

Stretching is important for healing. To reach up. To reach out. To go beyond our self. In burnout we tend to *contract*. We become smaller. Strange, since we have the illusion of being bigger than life, more expansive, open and available. In reality our eco-systems shrink. We even become physically shorter as we burn out. Our horizons become small and we become the centre of the universe (although we have the illusion of being everything to everyone).

Body stretching is a good place to begin. Simply reach up, out, down. Put on some energetic music early in the day and begin to dance to it with two major icons before you: STRETCH/BREATHE. It will create very exciting energy for you as you greet the day. What a difference from the silent, coffee mug depressed picture we often associate with the morning. You can do that later, if you choose to do so, but begin with high energy movement. Try to stretch out every joint. Anything that has a hinge in your system should be stretched. IT ONLY TAKES A FEW MINUTES. It could give you many more years of vibrant life.

From about the age of 19 we begin to tighten up. It is really up to us to stay *fluid and flexible*. It is too easy to become *up tight*. It is sad but true when this term is used to describe a whole person, not just the body! Stretching your body will not only help you to loosen up your body. It will help loosen up your whole being, your whole eco-system.

Stretching goes beyond the body. It flows over into the mind and spirit of a person. How do you stretch your imagination? Do you read? Travel? Try new things? When did you last GO OUT to a play, a film that could cause you to stretch, meet new kinds of people. Are all your friends from *your tribe*? The same colour, the same nationality, the same sexual orientation? Stretch. I always try to keep a novel going so that new ideas, new personalities, new situations are before me. I try to read in a variety of languages so that new worlds open up to me. Remember, each language is a window to a new universe. Italians have an altogether different worldview than the Germans. Women have another worldview from men. Do you only read books written by men? By women? Do you subscribe to alternative press publications? Do you eat only at fast-food counters?

Are you open to new ways of accessing your spirit? Are you bound religiously to the point that you could not explore other ways? Some people would dis-allow themselves to do yoga, or meditation because their mother-religion has not had the imagination to go in that direction. Not every path is all-embracing. We live in a VERY LARGE WORLD. The Creator has given us many foods to taste.

One of the happiest gifts of my Dominican training was the introduction to yoga that fr. Roger Paquet O.P. offered us as novices. Every morning before the 11:30 Conventual Eucharist, the novices did yoga in their cells. I'll never forget the first time I looked through the letter-opening in his door to find this exciting little man in shorts standing on his head in prayer. I called some others to witness the picture. He was a true instrument of freedom for us.

Dom Dechanet O.S.B. has written a book on Christian yoga. It might be a *way in* for those of you who are unable to explore the Eastern way directly.

8. Feel

Alexander Lowen says that "depression is caused by the suppression of emotion." He also says that "the depressive reaction may develop so insidiously that by the time it is full blown the person may have forgotten the specific event that triggered it." To get at the *core grief* is one thing. To get it EXPRESSED is totally another. The person who is tied up in burnout is often unable to express much with respect to his own life experience. Often the feelings have been so frozen or stuffed for so long that expression is impossible. I have found the approach of *bioenergetics* to be the best for the healing of burnout because it is a physical way to access the inner truth. It allows the person to proclaim "NO" with all the rage and power that he or she can muster in a world where "YES" is seen as the only legitimate way to respond to life.

We often are able to verbalize our feelings in an intellectual fashion but for true systemic healing, they must be *expressed OUT LOUD to someone.* Anything that can facilitate that happening in a safe environment is valuable. Although Lowen's bioenergetic approach is not the most popular therapeutic approach today, I believe that it is one of the most effective ways to access the heavily denied pain that burnout involves. We have been so trained to "control our emotions" that when our healing requires us to "control our reason and let our emotions out" we go into panic. A skilled therapist can serve as a "midwife" to help us *express* our inner pain.

9. Work

Sometimes people become so obsessed with their job that they forget who they are and who they want to be in the bigger picture. It is not only good to work, it is necessary. But when work becomes one's *total definition* it becomes a *spiritual disease*. Burnout ensues. One loses one's soul. Matthew Fox talks about JOB and WORK.

> "Jobs are to work as leaves are to a tree. If the tree is ailing the leaves will fall. Fiddling with leaves is not going to cure an ailing tree; just as one cures an ailing tree by treating its roots, so we cure the crisis in work by treating the root meaning and purpose of work. We make jobs by strengthening our view of work, not by pasting leaves onto a tree. A critical understanding of work will give birth to jobs, but without the grounding that a theology of work can provide us, jobs themselves will continue to dry up, just as do leaves on a dying tree."

Mathew Fox, THE REINVENTION OF WORK

Workaholism glues us and all our energy to a variety of jobs that seem never-ending and whose presence and constant call distract us from our *great work in the universe*. We get tied up in tasks-without-end rather than putting honest and vital energy into our true work which we never get to. To do that which we are truly called to do would not lead to burnout. The addictive environment (in which so many work) dis-allows the question of "vocation" to be a concern. Most people work in order to keep *someone else's* system going. They give up their soul in honour of *someone else's* dream or disease.

I have found in so many of my clients that they have awakened after a long sojourn in distress to the realization that they "prostituted" their lives to institutions which betrayed them in the end. This resulted in a deep sense at mid-life that they had no identity beyond the institution, no being that was their own and no reasonable rewards for their prostitution. They had been used and were spent. They sold their souls for security, prestige and a happy retirement. Now they had none of that. For some, it has been the end and they have sunk into a deep despair that is a near-death. Others, however, have been able to identify the demons and are able, at long last, to embrace their *true work* in the universe for the remainder of their lives. Some have even been able to build on the merits of the dysfunctional organization and use that as food for the future. Awakening from sleep is wonderful when the nightmare is understood. Some decide to live in grief and give more power to the nightmare than it merits.

10. Find An Elder

In addition to possibly having a therapist, have an elder. This could be your therapist. But not necessarily. Look for someone who has the goods to journey with you. Look for someone who has claimed his own story and is willing to share it with you. Here is an old tale by Ramakrishnan that might remind you of what a gift that *someone* could be.

> *Once upon a time there was an orphaned tiger cub. His mother had been killed by hunters. He was found by a herd of goats and raised with their young to believe that he too was a goat.*

> *One day the goats were out in the jungle, grazing in a clearing when in stalked a great king tiger. His fierce roar terrified the goats who ran off into the surrounding jungle. Suddenly the tiger cub, who thought he was a goat, found himself in the presence of the king tiger.*

> *At first, the tiger cub was afraid and could only bleat and sniff in the green grass. But then he discovered that, although he was afraid, yet he was not afraid - at least not like the others who had run off to hide.*

> *The great tiger, realizing that the cub imagined himself to be a goat, took him by the scruff of the neck and carried him to a pond. On the clear surface of the pond, the cub would be able to see that he was like the great tiger. But all the cub did when he saw their images side by side was to bleat goatwise in a question-ing and frightened way. Then the king tiger made one last effort to show the cub who thought he was a goat who he really was.*

He put before the cub a piece of meat. At first, the cub recoiled from it with horror. But then, coming closer he tasted it. Suddenly his blood was warmed by it. And the tiger cub who thought he was a goat lifted his head and set the jungle echoing with a mighty roar.

An elder is *one of the tribe*. An elder is one who has lived the journey.

An elder is one who has been valued in the human community. I would always look for someone whose scars were not too hidden.

The elder has the right story for each situation. This can have its source in mythology (the basis of psychiatric praxis) or in the elder's own life repertoire. This requires that he know the ancient wisdom of the human community. This allows him to know *from within* the various passages, deaths and resurrections that people normally go through in life.

The elder should be one who is in communion with the creative source of the universe. Someone who has no spirituality is likely not much better than a "mechanic" in the healing process - no matter what degrees he holds. In order to help the client recover his soul, the healer must *understand and respect* the reality of spirituality. The elder needs vibrant energy in order to help tackle this "inner death" and to re-vitalize the broken down.

The elder should also have an understanding that grief and pain are a normal part of the life-cycle and not an abnormality or an aberration. He should be someone with ears to hear, eyes to see, words to speak and arms to hold. The elder should be skilled in the language of the griever and be able to assure him that he is being heard correctly. The elder should be able to welcome *any pain*. No pain is invalid or wrong. The elder has no business making moral judgements about anyone's grief. The elder's job is to receive the story, honour it and continue from there.

Lastly, the elder should know joy and exhibit signs of radiance and delight. When you are looking for someone to be your elder, don't expect positive energy from someone who has little happy spirit.

11. Contemplate

In the words of David Suzuki in an article in the TORONTO STAR, we should initiate the new members of the human community into an understanding that we are *a part of and not above* the earth, our fragile island home. We must change from looking upon ourselves as the centrepiece of creation to the realization that we have *only recently* emerged from the web of living things *to which we remain interconnected.* We must learn to develop a long term harmony with nature rather than have immediate gratification through economic growth and consumption. So that the generations to come might have a future, we must change from being dominant and controlling to being inter-dependent and sharing. We must respect and reverence all life forms. Our own species' needs must be in harmony with other species' needs. We must move from individual self interest to community and cooperation.

This requires DEEP CONVERSION. I believe that deep personal and communal transformation is necessary if we are to make it beyond the next few decades. This cannot just come about by DOING. I believe we need to learn to BE. To BE ALONE. Then to PRACTICE BEING TOGETHER.

In the post-Cartesian period we have had few supports for this kind of world-vision. Even Church which proclaims the communion of all peoples has modeled ego-centric as opposed to eco-centric and global spirituality. The more fundamentalist the religious practice these days, the more self-centred it seems to be. We need to be truly *catholic* i.e. universal, for our race to survive into the third millennium.

12. Journal

The image I have of people who are burnout-prone is one of an eager but energy-less body being pulled forward by an over-zealous, over-wound up mind. People who live *beyond* themselves little by little lose themselves. Journalling is one way to recover who you are and what you do. To sit every day and recover what has been lived, not only capturing the events but also the motivations behind one's actions can be a most beneficial activity. Introverts are more inclined to do this sort of activity. Extroverts could try talking into a microphone or sharing their day with an intimate friend. Regardless, I believe the exercise and discipline of writing daily in a bound book is of great benefit. For those who cannot imagine this, Ira Progoff's methods might be of some help. There are many good journalling sources. I have suggested John Cheever's journals in the bibliography because they show a life-in-development and will model excellent writing skills as well. He revealed some of his insights in the New York Times. You likely will not want to do the same. Who knows? You might discover that you CAN write or at least that you *like* to write.

With my students and clients I have also found the practice of life-chronology to be beneficial. This is a good way to re-capture your entire life. In a primary moment, you might enter the events as you remember them - keeping at least two pages per year of your life. In a second moment you might be able to re-cover some of your feelings around major events. This will certainly facilitate any work you might eventually do with a therapist or elder. Leaving the extra page allows you to *fill in the blanks* as you recall events later on. You will be amazed that the periods of your life that you have forgotten or blocked out often rush back in once the shuffle has begun to take place. You might also procure some zip-lock plastic bags and sort out your old family pictures in periods of time (infancy, early childhood, adolescence, etc.) These will certainly trigger memories. Look at your face in various poses at various times in your life. It often becomes quite clear that you were content or in great pain.

Recovery is a gift. It is a great heritage to leave the generation that follows us - the gift of YOUR life re-covered, un-covered and claimed. It is also a terrific gift to yourself.

13. Take The Phone Off The Hook

For most of us, this act constitutes "guerilla tactics". We feel that people have the *right* to get through to us at every moment of the day. No, they don't! We are private individuals who may allow someone to break through to us if we so desire.

When I lived at Blackfriars, the Dominican Priory at Oxford, I was stunned one day by a notice on the front door to the monastery. It was summertime and many of the brothers were absent. The sign read:

> If you ring the doorbell and there is no answer, please be patient.
> If, after 10 minutes no one comes to the door, do please leave us
> a note and if no one contacts you, you might return another day.

Needless to say, this blew my North American socks off. I had never imagined that one would not answer the door or be "on call" at all times for anyone. This is what we have to learn. Most of us are NEVER on call for ourselves or for our intimates. One day the brothers in my priory suggested that if they were to dress as laypeople and arrive at the priory door they would get to see me immediately but as brothers they had a harder time to get an *audience*. I think they knew that it was harder yet for Kelly to get an audience with Kelly for Kelly! Take the phone off the hook and perhaps you can enter into the spirit of renewed life that these suggestions offer.

14. Sparkle

Most of us live the first 40 years of *our* life for someone else. It very often takes a breakdown of some sort to give us the impetus to look at our journey as *ours*. Others come and go. With my various changes in life (which have been awful and wonderful and *mine*), I have been the "headliner" for a bit each time. But as soon as the next bit of news hits town, I'm off the hook. Nobody died because of my changes. I could have and they would all have gone on happily ever after. I once told my therapist that I had spent all my life trying to live up to my step-father's expectations of me. She asked me what they were. I cried as I said, "I DON'T KNOW!"

To find one's passion, one's bliss, is paradise. All we can ever build on with regards to the Creator's dream for us is *hunch, inkling*. These are great English words. They are about the deep mysteries that linger in our bowels about who we are to be for this time of the creation. This is *first* about WHO I AM TO BE FOR **MYSELF**. I am the first one who should *enjoy* my bliss. It is gift FOR ME.

This takes intense energy applied to listening to one's own soul. Often we don't allow this until we've realized that listening to others' scripts *for us* just doesn't work *for us*. How happy our children would be if we would encourage them to practice this discipline from the early days of their life. I never learned to play *Kelly* on the piano. I was only allowed to play Bach and Mozart and Chopin. Even though I make my living playing Kelly now, there is still a feeling of inferiority and unworthiness about not being a concert pianist and playing *someone else's music*. So it is with so many of our lives. We play other people's scripts and live in sad unfulfilledness and then die. What a pity!

This exercise can begin by asking what your *excite* is. What have you dreamed of being/doing in your wildest imagination? We forget that our imagination is as valid and vital as is our reason. No one ever told us to "Control your reason!" No, it was always, "Control your emotions!" And, like obedient children, we did and often lost our imagination in the process. It is time to get it back!

Let me share with you two stories.

(i)   My first "big" concert after leaving the Order was at the St. Lawrence Centre in Toronto. It was a wonderful night. The hall was sold out a week in advance. John Arpin had pulled together a marvellous string quartet for me. They played a few selections to warm up the audience as I sat in the dressing room. The makeup person had done a good job on me. I looked great. I felt great. My name was on the door. The house was enthusiastic. For one of the first times of my life I felt as though I was "in alignment" with myself. This was where I was meant to be. Bliss! Suddenly it hit. "You're fat. You're stupid. Who do you think you are, anyway? Why don't they all go home? You're no good. You'll likely forget the words." Shame took over as it so often has in my life. But I went on. The show was good. At least they clapped!

The makeup artist had added a little sparkle to my eyelids. He told me that it would be great because when the spotlights hit my eyes, my eyes would sparkle. I needed that! After the show I asked a friend, "Did my eyes sparkle?" The reply was, "Yes.

Even when you *closed* them!"

(ii) A few years ago my friend Richard died. He had asked me a few years prior to his death if I would help him in that final dance. He had been one of my "kids" around the Priory and so it was difficult to witness the dying process of one so young and vibrant. He was one of those kids I knew would be a great man, even when he was in Grade One. He grew in wisdom and grace. He became the king, the warrior, the lover and the magician that Karl Jung talks about. He was a wonderful husband and father. He integrated all of his energies into a wonderful life.

I looked at him on his deathbed when he was in a deep coma. This young man had captured the "sparkle" of life. He had told me often that my "sparkle" had sparked his soul. I know from his funeral and wake that his "sparkle" had touched the souls of many of his peers.

I leaned over Richard the day he died and said to him, "Rich, there are a lot of angels here. I told them to get here for you. Lay back. Let them look after you for a change. You can go now. It's time! I wrote a song for you last night. I want to sing it for you."

So I whispered the song into his ear. Tears rolled down his cheeks. He opened his eyes out of the coma and said, "I love you." He died that day. But the "sparkle" continues.

I want to share this song with you.

Take the time you need. Lay back. Let go of the things that impose themselves on you constantly. Just be for a bit. And let the angels look after *you* a bit, too...

Paradise˙

May the angels bear you gently
to the loving arms of God.
May they lead you to a new day
where the holy ones have trod.
May you dance with all the angels.
May you feast with all the saints.
May the God of all creation,
may the God of all the nations
hold you gently to his face.

May the God of all creation
hold you in his warm embrace.
May he welcome you as springtime -
see the radiance of your face.
May you feast with all the angels
in this festival of love.
May he welcome you back home
to happiness and love.

May the holy ones before us
lead you to the table there -
where there's food for all the people -
no more sorrow, no more cares.
May you see the God who made us -
tender, loving full of grace.
May you know the deepest joy
of dancing face to face.

Trust that the angels surround you in your journey from loss of soul
to integrated and joyful living. This is the gift of creation not just for
a few but for all of us.

May you learn that you can journey out of the pain that accompanies burnout into a time of peace and contentment.

May you grow to become an exciting old human, delightful within yourself - for your own pleasure. And through this journey towards wholeness, may you be an icon of hope for the children who follow you.

Loss of Soul:*burnout*

BIBLIOGRAPHY

Jeremiah Abrams, ed, *Reclaiming The Inner Child*, Los Angeles: Jeremy P. Tracher, 1990

Ernest Becker, *The Denial Of Death*, New York: Macmillan, 1975

Thomas Berry, *The Dream Of The Earth*, San Francisco: Sierra Club, 1988

Harold Bloomfield with Leonard Felder, *Making Peace With Your Parents*, New York: Ballantine Books, 1983

John Bradshaw, *Bradshaw On: The Family, A Revolutionary Way of Self Discovery*, Deerfield Beach, FL: Health Communications, 1988

____. *Healing The Shame That Binds You*, Deerfield Beach: Health Communications, 1988

____. *Homecoming*, New York: Bantam Books, 1990

William Bridges, *Transitions, Making Sense of Life's Changes,* Reading: Addison-Wesley, 1980

_____. *Managing Transitions, Making the Most of Change*, Reading: Addison-Wesley, 1991

Rita Nakashima Brock, *Journeys By Heart*, A Christology of Erotic Power, New York:Crossroads, 1987

Lucia Capacchione, *The Power Of Your Other Hand, A Course in Channeling the Inner Wisdom of the Right Brain*, North Hollywood: Newcastle, 1988

John Cheever, *The Journals Of John Cheever*, New York: Ballantine, 1991

M.D.Chenu, *The Theology Of Work: An Exploration*, Dublin: Gill and Son, 1963

Phil Cousineau, ed, *Soul, An Archeology*, San Francisco: Harper, 1994

Diane Fassel, *Working Ourselves To Death, And the Rewards of Recovery*, New York: Harper Collins, 1990

Merle Fossum, Marilyn Mason, *Facing Shame, Families in Recovery*, New York: Norton, 1986

Matthew Fox, *Whee! We, Wee All The Way Home, A Guide to the New Sensual Spirituality*, Gaithersburg: Consortium, 1976

_____. *The Reinvention Of Work, A New Vision of Livelihood for our Time*, San Francisco: Harper, 1994

Terence Fretheim, *The Suffering Of God*, Philadelphia: Fortress, 1984

Anodea Judith, *Wheels Of Life, A Users's Guide to the Chakra System*, St.Paul: Llewellyn 1989

Gershen Kaufman, *Shame, The Power of Caring*, Rochester VT: Shenkman, 1985

Bibliography

Sam Keen, *The Passionate Life, Stages of Loving*, New York: Bantam, 1983

____. *Fire In The Belly, On Being a Man*, New York: Bantam, 1991

____. *Inward Bound, Exploring the Geography of Your Emotions*, New York: Bantam, 1992

Laurel Elizabeth Keyes, *Toning, The Creative Power of the Voice*, Marina del Rey: DeVorss, 1973

Barbara Killinger, *Workaholics, The Respectable Addicts*, Toronto: Key Porter, 1991

Sheldon Kopp, *If You Meet The Buddha On The Road, Kill Him, The Pilgrimage of Psychotherapy Patients*, New York: Bantam, 1972

Alexander Lowen, *Depression And The Body, The Biological Basis of Faith and Reality*, New York: Penguin Books, 1972

Christina Maslach, *Burnout, The Cost of Caring*, Englewood Cliffs: Prentice Hall, 1982

Rollo May, *Love And Will*, New York: Dell, 1969

Alice Miller, *The Drama Of The Gifted Child*, New York: Meridian, 1983

____. *For Your Own Good, Hidden Cruelty in Child Rearing and the Roots of Violence*, New York: Meridian,1983

____. *Thou Shalt Not Be Aware, Society's Betrayal of the Child*, New York: Meridian, 1986

____. *The Untouched Key, Tracing Childhood Trauma in Creativity*, New York: Doubleday, 1990

Thomas Moore, *Care Of The Soul, A Guide for Cultivating Depth and Sacredness in Everyday Life*, New York: Harper Collins, 1992

____. *Soul Mates, Honoring the Mysteries of Love and Relationship*, New York: Harper Collins, 1994

Gerald O'Collins, *The Second Journey, Spiritual Awareness and the Mid-Life Crisis*, New York: Paulist Press, 1978

Anne Wilson Schaef, *Women's Reality, An Emerging Female System in a White Male Society*, Minneapolis: Winston, 1985

____. *Co-dependence: Misunderstood, Mistreated*, Minneapolis: Winston, 1985

____. *When Society Becomes An Addict*, San Francisco: Harper and Row, 1987

____. with Diane Fassel, *The Addictive Organization*, San Francisco: Harper and Row, 1988

____. *Escape From Intimacy, Untangling the "Love" Addictions: Sex, Romance, Relationships*, San Francisco: Harper and Row, 1990

____. *Beyond Therapy, Beyond Science, A New Model for Healing the Whole Person*, San Francisco: Harper and Row, 1992

Jonathan Schell, *The Fate Of The Earth*, London: Jonathan Cape, 1982

Dorothee Soelle and Shirley A.Cloyes, *To Work And To Love, A Theology of Creation*, Philadelphia: Fortress, 1984

Anthony Storr, *The Integrity Of The Personality*, Middlesex: Penguin, 1960

Claire Weekes, *Hope And Help For Your Nerves*, New York: Bantam, 1982

Charles Whitfield, *Healing The Child Within*, Deerfield Beach: Health Communication, 1989

_____. *A Gift To Myself, A Personal Workbook and Guide to Healing my Child Within*, Deerfield Beach: Health Communications, 1990

_____. *Co-dependence, Healing the Human Condition*, Deerfield Beach: Health Communications, 1991

_____. *Boundaries And Relationships, Knowing, Protecting and Enjoying the Self*, Deerfield Beach: Health Communications, 1993

Dwight Lee Wolter, *Forgiving Our Parents*, Minneapolis: CompCare, 1989

Marion Woodman, *Addiction To Perfection*, Toronto: Inner City Books, 1982

_____. *The Pregnant Virgin*, Toronto: Inner City Books, 1985

Loss of Soul:*burnout*